"David P. Hansen capture
conversation that is far past du
Hansen's book illumines the g........ and painstaking actions of the
church to recognize the harms inflicted throughout history and, more
importantly, harms being inflicted in this present moment. Without
recognizing the sinful motivations of a society built on exploitation,
true wellness and harmony cannot exist. *Native Americans, the Mainline
Church, and the Quest for Interracial Justice* is a vital first step in putting
together the pieces necessary for our society to achieve racial justice."

—Glen Chebon Kernell, Jr., Executive Secretary of Native
American & Indigenous Ministries, Justice & Relationships,
United Methodist Church

"*Native Americans, the Mainline Church, and the Quest for Interracial
Justice* is a stunning achievement! An insider to a mainline church,
David Phillips Hansen powerfully blends theological insight, rigorous
history, and personal experience to illuminate hard truths about
the church's often repressive interactions with Native Americans in
'Christianity's collusion with conquest.' But his account is far more
than critique. It is also a conceptually grounded, pragmatic call to the
church to engage with present-day Native Americans around acts of
reconstruction (fundamentally remaking relationships) and reparation
(repairing persisting cultural, economic, and land-related damage).
Moving all toward social healing through justice. Truly an essential
read for all concerned about indigenous peoples and social justice."

—Eric K. Yamamoto, University of Hawaii School of Law

"Churches who seek to become open to others are on the right
track, yet in order to make progress they need the guidance provided in
this book. Little will change without digging deep into our histories of
conflict, exploring genuine forms of non-patronizing relationships, and
fundamentally transforming both church and world in the encounter
with others. As the mainline begins to reshape its still troubled
relationships with Native Americans, many other relationships will be
reshaped as well."

—Joerg Rieger, Vanderbilt University, Author of *Unified We Are
a Force*

"David Hansen knows the white mainline church well enough to know that we have some confessing to do. At the top of the list is our shameful treatment of Native Americans, which is inseparable from our understanding of Protestant Christianity. Although our own denomination, the United Church of Christ, has made a formal apology, much more is needed to confront the cultural, economic, and political subjugation of Natives. This book provides both an analysis of our sin, and a way forward to redemption."

—Robin R. Meyers, Mayflower Congregational UCC Church, and Distinguished Professor of Social Justice, Oklahoma City University

"Having taught and worked cross-culturally in South Dakota for many years, I see clearly that the greatest obstacle to human progress everywhere is the failure to understand historical and contemporary contexts. This exceptional book provides those contexts remarkably well and argues compellingly for right action, speaking to the hearts and minds of people of all faith traditions. It should be required reading in seminaries and university courses and highly recommended to all readers."

—Charles L. Woodard, South Dakota State University, and Author of *Ancestral Voice: Conversations With N. Scott Momaday*

NATIVE AMERICANS, THE MAINLINE CHURCH, AND THE QUEST FOR INTERRACIAL JUSTICE

DAVID PHILLIPS HANSEN

chalice
press

Saint Louis, Missouri

An imprint of Christian Board of Publication

Copyright ©2016 by David Phillips Hansen.

All rights reserved. For permission to reuse content, please contact Copyright Clearance Center, 222 Rosewood Drive, Danvers, MA 01923, (978) 750-8400, copyright.com.

Biblical quotations are from the following:

The New Oxford Annotated Bible with the Apocrypha, Expanded Edition. Revised Standard Version. Containing the Second Edition of the New Testament and an Expanded Edition of the Apocrypha. Edited by Herbert G. May and Bruce M. Metzger. New York: Oxford University Press. Copyright © 1973, 1977 by Oxford University Press, Inc.

The Oxford Annotated Bible, Copyright © 1962 by Oxford University Press.

Revised Standard Version of the Bible, Old Testament Section, Copyright 1952; New Testament Section, First Edition, Copyright 1946; Second Edition © 1971 by Division of Christian Education of the National Council of Churches of Christ in the United States of America.

The Oxford Annotated Apocrypha, Copyright © 1965, 1977 by Oxford University Press, Inc.

The Apocrypha, Copyright © 1957; The Third and Fourth Books of the Maccabees and Psalm 151, copyright © 1977 by Division of Christian Education of the National Council of Churches of Christ in the United States of America.

A percentage of the author's royalties will be contributed to the Eagle Butte Learning Center in support of its mission.

Print: 9780827225282 EPUB: 9780827225299 EPDF: 9780827225305

Printed in the United States of America

This book is dedicated to the Eagle Butte Learning Center

The Eagle Butte Learning Center (EBLC) for American Indian pastors and lay leaders is a ministry of the Council for American Indian Ministry of the United Church of Christ. Located in Eagle Butte, South Dakota on the Cheyenne River Sioux Reservation, EBLC is strategically and geographically placed where it is accessible to reservation pastors and lay leaders. The mission is to offer an education that is theologically and culturally relevant to reservation pastors, particularly the Lakota pastors of Dakota Association in South Dakota where the largest concentration of American Indian United Church of Christ churches are located. Educators, theologians, and pastors who come to teach are carefully selected for their cultural competency or their potential for cultural relevancy; most of them have doctorates in their fields of study. Together, all are learners and teachers.

Because of dire finances and complicated family situations, educational events are offered to pastors, lay leaders, and often their families in the form of weekend retreats and workshops. Pastors and lay leaders select the subjects of retreats and workshops that would help them. The staff finds faculty who can address the requested subjects. Small grants, gifts, and memorials are used to provide meals, lodging, and transportation for the students, and the faculty are asked to donate their time and travel.

The Eagle Butte Learning Center is unique in every way!

Contents

Acknowledgments

I appreciate the hard work of many who helped me bring this book to completion. Jean Roth Jacobs, Phyllis Cole-Dai, Charles McCollough, and Rosemary McCombs Maxey read early drafts of this manuscript and gave me valuable advice and encouragement. I am grateful for the support of these friends.

Much closer to the date of publication, Michael Austin, Provost of Newman College, Wichita, Kansas, gave me helpful suggestions. Joerg Rieger, the Wendland-Cook Professor of Constructive Theology at Southern Methodist University, generously offered to read portions of my manuscript, as did George Tinker, Clifford Baldridge Professor of American Indian Cultures and Religious Traditions at Iliff School of Theology, Denver, and pastor of Living Waters Episcopal/Lutheran Indian Ministries in Denver. Professor Rieger also recommended that I contact Chalice Press, now my publisher. The members of Pine Valley Christian Church (Disciples of Christ), Wichita, Kansas, and Brookings United Church of Christ, South Dakota, gave me time to write while I served these congregations. I owe a special debt of gratitude to my editorial consultant, Professor Charles Woodard, Professor of English at South Dakota State University, Bookings, and to Ulrike Guthrie, my editor.

Kekapa Lee and Kimo Mersberger graciously shared their wisdom with me when I lived in Hawai'i. They deepened my appreciation of indigenous cultures and my understanding of the role of Christian missionaries in the Pacific region. A special word of thanks goes to the people of the Eagle Butte Learning Center, South Dakota, who helped me better understand the history of the Indian boarding schools from a Native American perspective. I have dedicated this book to Eagle Butte Learning Center.

I owe a debt of gratitude to Eric K. Yamamoto, Professor of Law at the William S. Richardson School of Law, University of Hawai'i, Manoa, whose book *Interracial Justice: Conflict & Reconciliation in Post-Civil Rights America* provided a framework for this book.

Most of all I am grateful for the support and encouragement of my partner of fifty years, Sally Duckworth Hansen.

PART ONE

Beginning

1

An Introduction

Mainline Protestant Christianity[1] in the United States cannot be fairly interpreted without understanding its interaction with Native Americans (hereafter sometimes shortened to Native(s), Indian(s), or indigenous peoples).[2] Similarly, the rapacious nature of white America's treatment of the nation's Native American population cannot be explained adequately without reference to Christianity. My more limited focus is mainline Protestant Christianity. Unfortunately, this aspect of religious life in U.S. history[3] is often not well understood.[4] Those of us who are white and who are members of the mainline church, as I am, must understand the church's contribution to our nation's anti-indigenous past, so that we can contribute to the creation of a more just and peaceful multicultural society in the future.

Mainline denominations represent the oldest branches of Protestantism in the United States. Although the influence of the mainline church has declined since the end of World War II, H. Richard Niebuhr, a prominent twentieth-century theologian in the mainline church, in lectures given in 1936 at Harvard Divinity School and the next year at Chicago Theological Seminary asserted: "Protestantism is American's 'only national religion and to ignore this fact is to view the country from a false angle.'"[5]

Today mainline denominations are ecumenically oriented. They often self-identify as progressive on human rights and matters of social justice. They tend to interpret the Bible in a historical-metaphorical way, rather than a literal-factual way.[6] Since I am not interested in analyzing individual denominations or making comparisons among them, I use the collective term "mainline church." When I cite the actions of a particular denomination, it is for illustrative purposes.

Mainline Protestant Christianity has been a crucial contributor to the Anglo-European cultural, economic, and political exploitation and subjugation of Native Americans since the founding of the Jamestown colony in 1607. The situation began to change in 2003, when the United Church of Christ self-identified as the first mainline denomination to apologize to Native Americans for its participation in running Indian boarding schools and those harmed by them. Since 2003 other mainline denominations have issued their own apologies.

These apologies signal a desire on the part of the mainline church to end the longest war one people has waged upon another in the history of the world—the Anglo-Christian war on Native Americans. They are also an opportunity for the church to reform itself and to define a new role for itself in our national life. But without the nourishment of a new vision and a vibrant theology that connects this vision to its mission, the energy behind the church's apology likely will either dry up or be displaced by competing priorities.

Knowing Our History, Defining Our Mission

We investigate our history not for the purpose of blaming our forebearers for their deeds, but rather so that we might free ourselves from their myopia and thereby prepare ourselves for the work before us. Whereas the former mission of the church to "civilize and Christianize Indians" was complicit with the Anglo-European invasion of the territories of Native Americans and the westward expansion of the United States, the apology offers the church the possibility to undertake a future mission that is consistent with the pursuit of interracial justice in a multicultural society. The postapology church could become an important ally in what I believe may be the most significant civil rights struggle of this century: namely, the Native American drive for self-governance.

To fulfill the promise of the apology, we first must and analyze the root causes of Christian anti-Native actions and attitudes. Only then can the church fully commit itself to the urgent task of building a more just and peaceful multicultural society in which the rights of Native Americans, other people of color, and non-Christian peoples are equally respected and honored.

My task is twofold: first, to expose and deconstruct the causes of the church's war on indigenous cultures; and second, to identify and define key theological, political, and economic foundations for the church's reformation that will prepare it for our multicultural future. Only by knowing and owning our history can those of us who are white members of the mainline churches be set free from the history of colonial (in contrast to postcolonial) Christianity and be empowered to create a new identity and a new mission for a church that we cherish.

The United Church of Christ's 2003 apology to Native Americans said in part:

> WHEREAS, the American Missionary Society and the American Board of Commissioners of Foreign Mission com-missioned missionaries who were zealous in their beliefs that

Indians had no religion and no souls and were therefore ripe for conversion to Christianity; and

WHEREAS, in the decade following 1869 the Christian denominations began to establish boarding schools with the underlying policy "to kill the Indian and save the man," and

WHEREAS, the boarding school was of paramount significance in the attempted genocide of an entire people, and the mandatory placement of Indian children in the boarding schools resulted in the loss of hundreds of languages, spiritual beliefs, traditional practices, and the destruction of healthy family life;....

THEREFORE, LET IT BE RESOLVED, that the United Church of Christ be the first church denomination to acknowledge, confess and accept its historic participation and accountability for the harm done through the establishment of boarding schools in the United States.[7]

The apology went on to commit the church to work with Native American communities within the denomination and with other communities of indigenous peoples and other allies to combat racial stereotyping, to oppose the subjugation and exploitation of Natives, and to end the destruction of indigenous cultures.

The 1893 World Parliament of Religions is indicative of the ethnocentrism of the mainline church and its disparagement of Native Americans.[8] The Parliament was a central feature of the World's Columbian Exposition, which was held in Chicago. The purpose of the Exposition was to celebrate the quadricentennial of the "discovery" of America by Christopher Columbus. The Parliament brought together thousands of people representing a broad spectrum of the world's diverse faith traditions, but U.S. Protestant Christianity was the main focus of the gathering. While the two African Americans invited to speak to the Exposition openly challenged the triumphal theology of the event, Native Americans were conspicuously not invited to participate. Their presence was limited to mock "Indian villages" intended to represent the evolutionary hierarchy of cultures from the primitive pagan past to the sophisticated and spiritually more enlightened Christian present.

The Columbian Exposition was an unabashed celebration of the ascendance of European and U.S. culture over all other cultures and of the superiority of Protestant Christianity over all other faith traditions. In the spirit of the times, a new magazine, *The Christian Century*, was launched in 1902. It quickly became the flagship publication of the mainline church. White Protestant America heralded the advent of the twentieth century as the dawn of the golden age of liberal Protestant Christianity in what promised to be the American century.

The banner of Protestant and U.S. hegemonic power did not unfurl as the turn-of-the-century visionaries expected, however. Today we live in a global village of many colors and many faiths. The apologies of the mainline churches to Native Americans are recognitions by these denominations of this reality. When these denominations issued their apologies, they renounced and formally terminated their historic mission to "civilize and Christianize the Indians." A growing number of denominations has since formally repudiated the long-standing and religiously sanctioned Doctrine of Discovery, which even now serves as the legal basis for federal claims to Native American land. It is difficult to overstate the importance of these actions of renunciation and repudiation, or the opportunity they present for the church to reinvent itself.

These acts of renunciation and repudiation indicate to me that we are entering what Lewis S. Mudge, then Professor of Systematic Theology at San Francisco Theological Seminary, called a "post-Westphalian world."[9] In Germany, the Peace of Westphalia, signed in 1648, marked the beginning of the modern secular state. It created a basis for national self-determination by granting the prince the exclusive right to tax citizens of the realm and to raise an army. It also incorporated the principle of *cuius region eius religio* ("whoever the prince may be, his will be the prevailing religion"), which was established earlier in the Peace of Augsburg, signed in 1555. The latter agreement also granted freedom of religion to subjects who did not wish to conform to the prince's choice. We can trace the origin of the doctrine of the separation of church and state and the rise of denominational Protestantism to these two accords.

After 1648, nationalism gradually replaced religion as the focus of people's loyalty and identity. Subsequently Christian theology and church became located in the "force fields" of the state but not co-opted by it completely.[10] On one level, there was a widely shared assumption in Western circles that the growing power of the nation-state would be beneficial for Christianity and that Christianity would be beneficial for the state. On another level, religious freedom meant that faith increasingly "became marginalized, privatized, and individualized in both its conception and its content."[11]

The mainline church's renunciation of its historic mission to "civilize and Christianize Indians" and its repudiation of the Doctrine of Discovery indicate that we are approaching the end of the world started by the Peace of Westphalia and the church's role in it. As such, the church has an opportunity to claim a less culturally compromised identity and to proclaim a less privatized understanding of the gospel.

A Personal Story

A few years after the United Church of Christ's 2003 apology, Reverend Rosemary McCombs Maxey, an Oklahoma pastor of the Muscogee Creek Nation, invited me to attend a weekend pastors' class held at the Eagle Butte Learning Center in South Dakota. During a conversation with the Reverend Norman Bluecoat, a pastor and member of the Cheyenne River Sioux Tribe, he observed that white Christians often expressed hope for reconciliation with Native Americans. Then Bluecoat told me: "We can never be reconciled. Reconciliation assumes that we were once together. We have never been together."

"Never" implies permanence. As Bluecoat knows, there were times in the past when indigenous peoples and settlers did cooperate. Today every mainline denomination has a Native American ministry in some form. However, historically the church's mission to Native Americans was not guided by a desire to protect indigenous cultures or to advocate for indigenous peoples' right of self-determination. With some exceptions, the church's history has been shaped both by misunderstanding of Native American cultures and mistrust of Native American peoples, as well as by goals of extermination or assimilation. Can we change this pattern? The hope expressed in the United Church of Christ apology is that we can create a climate of mutual respect and understanding in order to create a more just and people-oriented society.

I owe Bluecoat and McCombs Maxey a debt of gratitude. In some respects this book is my response to Bluecoat's comment, an outgrowth of my experiences at the Eagle Butte Learning Center and my tenure in South Dakota, where I served as the interim pastor of the Brookings United Church of Christ. Members of that congregation and friends at South Dakota State University enriched my understanding of Native American cultures and history.

My family also prepared me for this work. My immediate family includes blacks and whites, Christians, Muslims, and atheists. We are an interracial and interfaith family. We are not all U.S. citizens, although we all live in the United States. The issues that I wrestle with in this book are personal.

My lifetime in the mainline church has also taught me valuable lessons that prepared me for writing this book. I grew up in a white Anglo-Saxon Protestant church and culture. As a child I believed in the twin myths of the great American melting pot and America's manifest destiny. I had the good fortune of attending and graduating from the Pacific School of Religion (PSR) in Berkeley, California. Later I returned to Berkeley and attended the Graduate Theological Union (GTU), where I earned my doctor of philosophy, specializing in the field of religion and society with a focus on economics. The GTU is a consortium of theological schools and institutes that is as rich a multicultural, interfaith, cosmopolitan environment as one can find anywhere. My experiences at both PRS and the GTU prepared me for the future in ways that I could not fully appreciate at the time.

I was in seminary when the Indians of All Tribes occupied Alcatraz Island on November 20, 1969. The occupation lasted eighteen months before the federal government forcibly ended it on June 11, 1971. Roxanne Dunbar-Ortiz, the daughter of a Cherokee mother and a Scots-Irish father, reports in *An Indigenous Peoples' History of the United States* that the thriving island village drew Natives from across the continent and radicalized thousands of youth.[12] She tells us that in addition to issuing the "Proclamation of the Indians of All Tribes" to the U.S. government, in which the Indians offered to form a "bureau of Caucasian Affairs," the group made serious demands for four institutions to be established on Alcatraz: a Center for American Indian Studies; an American Indian Spiritual Center; an Indian Center for Ecology; and a Great Indian Training School. They also demanded that a memorial be created to be a reminder that once the island had been a prison used to incarcerate and execute those Native Americans in California who resisted the United States. These institutions were later established on land near the campus of the University of California, Davis, which was the first university to offer a doctorate in Native American studies.[13] Looking back, I believe the occupation of Alcatraz Island was as galvanizing an event for raising national consciousness about Native American civil rights as the 1965 March to Selma was for the voting rights movement.

Upon graduation from seminary, I served as a campus minister at the University of Saskatchewan, Saskatoon, Canada. I am forever grateful to Canadian friends for giving me this opportunity to learn about First Nations peoples and the United Church of Canada. I examine the apology of the United Church of Canada to First Nations peoples in chapter eight, and contrast it to the actions of the mainline churches in the United States.

After a brief time in Canada, I served in parish ministry in various locations in the United States. I was also the Conference Minister of the Hawai'i Conference of the United Church of Christ and the Conference Minister of the Kansas-Oklahoma Conference of the United Church of Christ. In addition, I have served on regional, ecumenical, and interfaith bodies and national church boards and participated in a number of international delegations. I traveled to Chiapas, Mexico, in the spring of 1995, not long after the Zapatista Uprising, and met Bishop Samuel Ruiz. Like Bartolomé de las Casas, who in the sixteenth century became the first bishop of Chiapas, Bishop Ruiz is a strong defender of the rights of indigenous peoples.

In short, the struggle of indigenous peoples for self-governance is global and ongoing. What happens here in the United States is not isolated.[14]

My first direct experience with an apology by the church happened when I was in Hawai'i. In 1993 the United Church of Christ issued a formal apology to *kanaka Maoli* (Native Hawaiians) for the complicity of its predecessor denomination, the Congregational Christian Church, in the overthrow of the Hawaiian monarchy in 1893. In addition to the formal apology, the church gave a significant amount of money to *kanaka Maoli* congregations that remained part of the denomination following the overthrow and transferred valuable land on each of five islands to *kanaka Maoli*. It also created and partially funded a new ethnically defined Hawaiian Association that was and is a semiautonomous body governed by *kanaka Maoli*.[15] As part of the apology, the denomination contributed $1.5 million to a newly created independent foundation for the benefit of the Hawaiian community.

I moved to Hawai'i in 1995 to become a member of the Hawai'i Conference staff, and the pastor of Koloa Union Church on the island of Kauai. Two years later, in 1997, the final payments associated with the Hawaiian Apology were made and the land transfers were completed. Soon after these transactions were concluded, I became the conference minister of the Hawai'i Conference.

The church's apology to *kanaka Maoli* caused me to reassess the missionary history of the church not only in Hawai'i but throughout the Pacific. It also forced me to examine the relationship between the Hawai'i Conference and *kanaka Maoli* who remained part of the church and between the Conference and *kanaka Maoli* who rejected the church. The emerging Hawaiian Sovereignty movement helped me begin to understand the ambiguous role of religion as a force both for oppression and for liberation.

Ten years after the apology to *kanaka Maoli*, in 2003 the United Church of Christ apologized to Native Americans for its participation in the history of Native genocide. I was the conference minister of the Kansas-Oklahoma Conference of the United Church of Christ at the time. My experience in Hawai i gave me a unique perspective on the strengths and shortcomings of the church's apology to Native Americans.

That the apology to Native Americans took place encouraged me, but that it was such a timid apology disheartened me. It included neither the payment of significant funds nor the transfer of land. No independent self-governing Native American judicatory was established. No foundation was endowed. The apology did not provide for any deep structural changes in the power dynamics of the church. In short, the apology to Native Americans confirmed my suspicion that the general attitude of many well-intentioned white people in the church toward Native Americans lacked a deep understanding of the history of the church and its anti-Native past.

Today I am cautiously hopeful for the church. The apology to Native Americans is significant. Subsequent actions taken by the church are important. Yet, to paraphrase Robert Frost's poem "Stopping by Woods on a Snowy Evening," we "have promises to keep,/ And miles to go before [we] sleep."[16]

A Qualifying Disclaimer and Challenge

I conclude this introduction with a qualifying disclaimer and a challenge. I do not claim extensive knowledge of Native American history or tribal cultures, the law, economics, or many other fields that I explore. My experience is that of a white person who has served in a variety of leadership positions in one denomination, the United Church of Christ. I am undertaking this project as an independent religious scholar who is thankful for the scholarship and expertise of others. My intention is to use their work faithfully and with integrity. If there are errors in this book, they are mine alone.

I have written this book because I believe that there is a real-world urgency for the church to be about the work of interracial justice. It is time for the mainline church to help the United States become what Walt Whitman envisioned when he described our nation as "not merely a nation but a teeming nation of nations."[17] This is the challenge that awaits us.

NOTES

[1]The largest mainline denominations in the United States are United Methodist, Evangelical Lutheran Church in America, Presbyterian Church (USA), Episcopal Church, American Baptist Church in the USA, United Church of Christ, Christian Church (Disciples of Christ), and the Reformed Church in America. The Pew Forum on Religion and Public Life uses the term "Mainline Protestant Churches" to distinguish theses denominations from "Evangelical Protestant Churches," and "Historically Black Protestant Churches." See Pew Forum on Religion and Public Life/U.S. Religious Landscape Survey: Religious Beliefs and Practices: Diverse and Politically Relevant, June 2008. Appendix 3, "Classifications of Protestant Denominations," 167–73. http:// religions.pewforum.org/pdf/report2religious-landscape-study-appendix3.pdf. Accessed 07/07/2014.

[2]Charles C. Mann, *1491: New Revelations of the Americas before Columbus* (New York: Vintage Books, 2011), second edition. In Appendix A, "Loaded Words," Mann writes: "Anyone who attempts to write or even speak about the original inhabitants of the Americas quickly runs into terminological quicksand," 393. The Council for American Indian Ministries, United Church of Christ, prefers American Indians. Academic communities tend to use Native American. I use "Native American." For brevity I sometimes use "Native" or "Natives." I use "Indian" when called for by historical context, such as "Indian boarding school." I use national and tribal names, such as Cherokee Nation, and Muscogee Creek Nation, and Cheyenne River Sioux Tribe, when possible.

[3]See Roxanne Dunbar-Ortiz, *An Indigenous Peoples' History of the United States* (Boston: Beacon Press, 2014), xiv. She notes that "America" and "American" as commonly used are imperialistic terms. Therefore, I have limited my use of "America" and "American" in recognition of the fact that other people living in the Western hemisphere are also "American." I use "United States" as a noun, "U.S." as an adjective, and "white Americans" when referring to Caucasian citizens.

[4]Robert J. C. Young, *Postcolonialism: An Historical Introduction* (Oxford: Blackwell Publishing, 2001). The following are examples of the tendency to minimize the role of religion in the history of British conquest: "The Pilgrim Fathers were fleeing the established church, not sailing across the Atlantic on its behalf on an imperial mission." "Unlike the Spanish, the British and Dutch did not initially justify colonization in terms of Christian mission, though Protestant-Catholic rivalries between European powers provided a significant factor in the establishment or seizure of colonies. Colonization is often associated with notions of civilizing or missionary work but, aside from the Spanish and Portuguese expeditions to Central and South America, this cultural imperialism was really the later product of imperialism in its nineteenth century form," 16, 22.

[5]H. Richard Niebuhr, *The Kingdom of God in America* (New York: Harper & Row, Publishers, 1937, Harper Torchbook edition, 1959), 17. Niebuhr suggests that Puritanism was the main source of American religion in footnote 1, 199–200. Niebuhr cites André Siegfried, *America Comes of Age* (New York, 1927), as the source of this quotation, 33, fn. 2 on 200.

[6]Marcus J. Borg, *Reading the Bible Again for the First Time: Taking the Bible Seriously but Not Literally* (New York: HarperCollins Publishers, Inc., 2001), ix.

[7]Minutes of the Twenty-Fourth General Synod of the United Church of Christ, July 11–13, 2003, Mary Ann Murray and Nancy Cope, eds., "American Indian Boarding Schools," July 13, 2013, 41–42. www.uccfiles.com/synod/resolutions/AMERICAN-INDIAN-BOARDING-SCHOOLS.pdf. Accessed 5/13/2012.

[8]My source is the Boston Collaborative Encyclopedia of Western Theology, "World Parliament of Religion (1893)." Derek Michaud, ed., incorporating material by Joas Adoprasetya (2004), copyright by Wesley J. Wildman. http://people.bu.edu/wwildman/bce/worldparliamentofreligions1893.htm
Accessed 3/9/2015.

[9]Lewis S. Mudge, *The Church as Moral Community: Ecclesiology and Ethics in Ecumenical Debate* (New York: The Continuum Publishing Company and Geneva: WCC Publications, 1998). Mudge discusses the Peace of Westphalia and the post-Westphalian world, 36–41.

[10]See Joerg Rieger, "Christian Theology and Empires," in *Empire and the Christian Tradition: New Readings of Classical Theologians*, ed. Kwok Pui-lan, Don H. Compier, and Joerg Rieger (Minneapolis: Fortress Press, 2007), 1–13.

[11]Mudge, *Moral Community*, 38. Mudge cites Robert Bellah and Bryan Hehir as sources for this. See fn. 49, 171. See Robert N. Bellah, "How to Understand the Church in an Individualistic Society," in *Christianity and Civil Society*, ed. Rodney L. Peterson (Maryknoll, NY: Orbis Books, 1995), 4ff.

[12]Dunbar-Ortiz, *Indigenous Peoples*, 183–84.

[13]Ibid., 184.

[14]Linda Tuhiwai Smith, *Decolonizing Methodologies: Research and Indigenous Peoples* (London: Zed Books, Ltd., 1999, seventh impression, 2004). I was not able to incorporate Smith's insights because the present manuscript was completed before I was aware of her work, but I want to acknowledge this important book which documents the rise of indigenous scholarship and the global nature of indigenous peoples' drive for self-governance.

[15]Up until the time of the apology the Hawai'i Conference, like most mainline judicatories, was divided administratively into geographically defined regions variously

called "associations," "districts," or such. The new association was the first in the denomination to be defined by ethnicity rather than geography.

[16]Robert Frost, "Stopping By Woods on a Snowy Evening," in *A Pocket Book of Robert Frost's Poems* (New York: Washington Square Press, Inc., 1963), sixteenth printing, 194. The last lines of Frost's poem read: "The woods are lovely, dark and deep.' But I have promises to keep,/ And miles to go before I sleep,/ And miles to go before I sleep."

[17]Walt Whitman, "Preface 1855—*Leaves of Grass*, First Edition," in *Leaves of Grass and Other Writings of Walt Whitman*, ed. Michael Moon (New York: W.W. Norton & Company, 2002), 616.

2

Mapping the Terrain

In *Like a Loaded Weapon: The Rehnquist Court, Indian Rights, and the Legal History of Racism*, Robert A. Williams Jr., a member of the Lumbee Tribe and a legal scholar who served as a United Nations special rapporteur on the Rights of Indigenous Peoples, recalls a very telling *Far Side* cartoon by Gary Larson that depicts a Native dressed in buckskins and full feathered-headdress regalia standing next to a teepee, addressing members of his tribe.[1] The gathered Native Americans are also dressed in buckskin. They are either sporting feathers or wearing braids. The Native standing in front is obviously the leader. He is holding up a necklace made of some tacky beads. In the bubble above his head, he proudly proclaims, "To begin, I'd like to show you *this*! Isn't it a beaut'?" The caption below the cartoon reads, "New York 1626: Chief of the Manhattan Indians addresses his tribe for the last time."

In his commentary on this cartoon, Robert Williams says that it is rooted in the "commonly held, long-established negative racial stereotype about Indians in the America racial imagination."[2] Most people have heard stories about the dumb Native Americans selling the priceless real estate of Manhattan to the Dutch for worthless trinkets. At the same time, most people also know that the story is apocryphal. In a humorous way the cartoon exposes white people's tradition of racial profiling and the use of race-based stereotypes and denigrating racial imagery. We know that the story is not true; nonetheless the story does not go away. The image of a Native American in buckskin holding worthless trinkets aloft is securely deposited in our national memory bank.

Most people are well enough informed to understand Gary Larson's cartoon. What most people do not know is the terrain of history and religion in which these white stereotypes are rooted. Until we grapple with, investigate, and interrogate this well-established but largely hidden history, our hope for interracial justice and a more peaceful society will remain what it is today—a phantom wish for reconciliation.

We white Protestants must equip ourselves with the necessary intellectual tools for the work of deconstructing anti–Native American attitudes, so that we can provide leadership for the creation of a new social fabric that is life-giving for all people. We can recall elements in our biblical history which are profoundly critical of unjust and oppressive social structures. We can inspire hope through the use of appropriate religious stories, symbols, and rituals. We can use the considerable resources of the church to combat negative stereotyping and the display of denigrating images. Most important, we can take the high moral ground and attend to the "weightier matters of the law, justice and mercy and faith" (Mt. 23:23b).

Who Should Be Interested?

My immediate intended audiences include Christians—mainline, evangelical, and all others—and Native Americans. I hope that anyone interested in making a positive contribution to the pressing national conversation on religion, race, and interracial justice will find this book useful. I also hope that people concerned about the relationship between the church and the state will find this book helpful. People who want to perpetuate the oppression of Native Americans and the expropriation and exploitation of their homeland will not be sympathetic to my argument.

In a more general way I hope that historians, religious and race scholars, resolution practitioners, and others who are interested in rapprochement and interracial justice will find this book a useful resource. I think the book lends itself to use in college, university, and seminary classrooms where questions about religion, race, and multicultural justice are examined.

What Is Interracial Justice?

It is difficult to understand what "interracial justice" means when we do not have a common understanding of "race." I accept sociologist Beverly Daniel Tatum's definition of race as "a group that is socially defined on the basis of *physical* criteria" such as skin color and facial features.[3] People of European descent who have white or light skin color are "white people"; all others are "people of color." To say that the United States is a white racist society or that the mainline church is a white racist institution means that institutional power and patterns of social control are vested disproportionately in the hands of white people and used by white people for their own benefit. It does not mean that all white people are by definition racist.

To claim that mainline denominations are racist institutions means that racism is both a problem of white people and an institutional affliction. Racism is first and foremost a white problem because it is white people who benefit from it. It is an institutional problem because the purpose of white racism is to project and to protect white privilege and power. Discriminating against, negatively stereotyping, and otherwise marginalizing people of color are strategies of racism. Dismantling institutional racism means disarming and dismantling structures that project and protect white privilege and power.

Therefore, interracial justice is about more than being "fair," "giving each person her or his due," or even "treating equals equally," all of which are common definitions of justice. Interracial justice is about creating a *"people-oriented"* society, to use Paulo Freire's wonderful phrase.[4] To have faith means that we have hope that we can transform this offensive world into a *"people-oriented"* world and that we are ready to act on this hope.

Since the 1960s there has been growth in race theory and in our understanding of racism and other forms of discrimination. But it has been hard to crack institutional forms of racism rooted in white European and Christian values. We have not transferred the personal to the institutional and so have often ended up with well-intended but vague and misguided hopes for reconciliation.

We need to find a different way to investigate and disarm institutionally entrenched bigotry and racism. Simply stated, we have to end colonialism. Colonialism in all of its forms is fueled by assumptions about the innate moral, cultural, economic, intellectual, and political superiority of the colonizing power.[5] Protestantism legitimated and facilitated Anglo-American colonialism, and profited from it. What we need is a praxis, a theory and a method of action and reflection, to end colonialism.

Eric K. Yamamoto's groundbreaking book, *Interracial Justice: Conflict and Reconciliation in Post-Civil Rights America*, provides a suitable framework for ending Christian subjugation and exploitation of Native Americans.[6] Yamamoto invites us "to conceptualize, ruminate on, and act on grievances underlying present-day tensions," using "four praxis dimensions of combined inquiry and action." The first dimension is *recognition*—identifying disabling social constraints and resulting social wounds and justice grievances; and critically examining stock stories ostensibly legitimating the causes of the grievances. The second dimension is *responsibility*—assessing the social and economic conditions and the political alignments of power, and, when appropriate, accepting responsibility for healing wounds caused by the abuse of power. The third dimension is *reconstruction*—taking active steps by the aggressor to heal social and psychological wounds resulting from the abuse of power, and, when appropriate, asking for forgiveness. The fourth dimension is *reparation*—repairing the damage to the material well-being of racial group life in order to attenuate one group's power over another and to aid in rebuilding relationships.[7]

The Book's Design

This book is divided into four main parts, following the contours of interracial justice in Yamamoto's dynamic model. Part Two, *"Recognition,"* has three chapters. The first chapter, entitled "The European Foundations of Cultural Imperialism," identifies and examines important theological developments in medieval Europe and salient political events in the late Tudor and early Stuart monarchies in England that prepared the way for the Anglo invasion of what would become the United States. The next chapter, entitled "Coming to America," has three sections. In the first section, I examine the history of Jamestown, which at its inception the Church of England validated as a "holy experiment." In the second section, I focus on the Pilgrims and the Puritans and the founding of the Bible Commonwealth of New England. In the third section, I examine seventeenth-century military and cultural campaigns to dominate indigenous peoples and destroy their cultures. Chapter Five, "Christian Collusion with Western Colonialism," examines some of the key events in the period from the Great Awakening in the eighteenth century through the twentieth century. These events document how the church during this period confused the ways of Christ with the ways of Western culture. I also discuss the more recent rise of Native American resistance to internal colonialism.

Whereas Part Two analyzes the theological and political roots of the church's mission to civilize and Christianize indigenous peoples,, the chapters in Part Three, *"Responsibility,"* examine the interplay between theology and the social order. In chapter six, entitled "Christianity at a Crossroads," I decode the biblical story of the Exodus—the stock story (Yamamoto's phrase) that validated the Anglo invasion of North America and later contributed to the mythology that the United States was in its origin a white Christian nation. I argue that white Christians must learn to interpret this story from below—not as a story of promise-fulfillment, but rather as a story of liberation *and* conquest. In chapter seven, entitled "Images of God and Our Social Order," I turn my attention to our understanding of the character of God and investigate how our understanding of God validates our social order. I contend that we must move away from a conventional understanding of God as promise-maker and promise-keeper and adopt a more nuanced political theology that relates the character of God to the legitimation of a social structures, the reality of social injustices created by those structures, and the struggle to transform social structures in the interest of creating a more just society.

Part Four, "*Reconstruction*," is a single chapter, chapter eight, entitled "The Journey of Repentance." The first section of this chapter examines the apology of the mainline church to Native Americans and subsequent actions taken by the church. The second section focuses on the experience of the United Church of Canada, which has apologized to First Nations peoples for its participation in the history of indigenous genocide. The anti-indigenous history of the mainline church in the United States and the anti-indigenous history of the United Church of Canada parallel each other in many ways. I believe that the apology of the United Church of Canada, while different from that of the church in the United States, can be instructive for members of the mainline church.

Part Five, "*Reparation*," looks toward the future. I argue in chapter nine, "Economics in the Service of Life," that we measure only what we value. As long as there is a pronounced discrepancy between our professed moral values and the way we measure economic success, as there is today, we will find ourselves pulled in opposite directions, pursuing incompatible goals, and making unsatisfying compromises. In order to create an economy in the service of life, we need to adopt an economic metric that more clearly connects our moral values and our economic policies. Once we make this connection, we will be able to adopt appropriate economic and social policies based on the principles of well-being and interracial justice. Then the church will be better equipped to invest itself and its resources in building a people-oriented society.

Chapter ten, "A Theology of Land and of Life," focuses on a theology of the land and the stewardship of it. Control of the land is *the* central issue that defines the relationship between Euro-Americans and Native Americans. In order to pursue interracial justice, we *must* change our understanding of the institution of private property and the interests it serves. The chapter concludes with a parable of Jesus that reframes our traditional understanding of property, and prepares us for the next phase in the journey from Jamestown to Justicetown—my metaphor for our destination.

Defining Terms

Before proceeding further, it will be helpful to the reader if I clearly define three key and admittedly provocative concepts that I use throughout the book: "anti-Native," "genocide," and "deep solidarity."

Anti-Native

The term "anti-Native" draws on the work of Elizabeth Cook-Lynn, who coined the phrase "Anti-Indianism." She defines the traits of Anti-Indianism as: "the cause of unnatural deaths of Indians, the denigration of being an Indian in America, placing blame on Indians, and exploiting and distorting Indian cultures and beliefs."[8] She argues that it is "a fundamental element of American Christianity. She says that because indigenous America was not Christian it was seen as "an opposing force that had to be obliterated at any cost."[9]

Cook-Lynn contends that because anti-Indianism is rooted in religion, it has almost free reign in art, politics, and many other areas of American life. I am indebted to Cook-Lynn for her insightful analysis of Christianity, and the Anglo-Christian campaign against Native American peoples and cultures. For reasons explained in the appendix, I am using "anti-Native" rather than "Anti-Indian" throughout this text. Where possible I use indigenous names.

The destructive impact of White anti-Native bias is evident in this 1885 Proctor and Gamble ad for Ivory Soap:

> We were once factious, fierce and wild,
> In peaceful arts unreconciled
> Our blankets smeared with grease and stains
> From buffalo meat and settler's veins.
> Through summer's dust and heat content
> From moon to moon unwashed we went,
> But IVORY SOAP came like a ray
> Of light across our darkened way
> And now we're civil, kind and good
> And keep the laws as people should,
> We wear our linen, lawn and lace
> As well as folks with paler face
> And now I take, where'er we go
> This cake of IVORY SOAP to show
> What civilized my squaw and me
> And made us clean and fair to see.[10]

The ad's depiction of Native Americans as "fierce," "wild," and "unwashed" reinforces the image of a primitive and uncivilized people. The word "squaw" is taken from the Algonquin language. It means "woman" or "daughter."[11] It did not originally have a derogatory connotation. White society redefined "squaw" and gave it a pejorative and often sexual content.

Andrea Smith, a Cherokee scholar and activist, points out that the denigration of women of color is of particular importance to colonial powers because it is a strategic way to control, exploit, and degrade the cultures of people of color. Smith writes: "The project of colonial sexual violence established the ideology that Native bodies are inherently violable—and by extension, that Native lands are also inherently violable." She continues: "As a consequence of this colonization and abuse of their bodies, Indian people learn to internalize self-hatred, because body image is integrally related to self-esteem....When the bodies of Indian people are designated as sinful and dirty, it becomes a sin just to be Indian. Native peoples internalize the genocidal project through self-destruction."[12]

Anglo anti-Native prejudice is not only a way to control, exploit, and degrade Native Americans. It is also a way to project and protect white power and privilege as is evident in Walt Whitman's poem, "A Death Sonnet for Custer," written less than a month after Custer was killed in the Battle of Little Bighorn on June 26, 1876. The poem was first published in the *New York Daily Tribune*, July 10, 1876.[13]

I.

From far Montana's cañons,
Lands of the wild ravine, the dusky Sioux, the lonesome stretch,
     the silence,
Haply, to-day, a mournful wail—haply, a trumpet
     note for heroes.

II.

The battle-bulletin,
The Indian ambuscade—the slaughter and environment
The cavalry companies fighting to the last—in sternest, coolest,
     heroism.
The fall of Custer, and all his officers and men.

III.

Continues yet the old, old legend of our race!
The loftiest of life upheld by death!
The ancient banner perfectly maintained!
(O lesson opportune—O how I welcome thee!)
As, sitting in dark days,
Lone, sulky, through the time's thick murk looking
     in vain for light, for hope,
From unsuspected parts, a fierce and momentary
     proof,
(The sun there at the center, though concealed,
Electric life forever at the center,)
Breaks forth, a lightning flash.

IV.

Thou of sunny, flowing hair, in battle,
I erewhile saw, with erect head, pressing ever in
     front, bearing a bright sword in thy hand,
Now ending well the splendid fever of thy deeds,

(I bring no dirge for it or thee—I bring a glad, triumphal sonnet;)
There in the far northwest, in struggle, charge, and
    saber-smite,
Desperate and glorious—aye, in defeat most desperate, most
    glorious,
After thy many battles, in which, never yielding up
    a gun or a color,
Leaving behind thee a memory sweet to soldiers,
Thou yieldest up thyself.

Cook-Lynn says that Whitman, this most American of poets who is often cited and celebrated as a defender of freedom, wrote this "piece of propagandist history"[14] in order to make Custer—"Thou of sunny, flowing hair"—heroic and to portray Native Americans as unworthy of their victory.

But the truth is that Custer was not ambushed as the poem suggests. The Sioux and Cheyenne did not launch an unexpected attack. Custer had been pursuing them for hundreds of miles. He attacked the Natives with the single goal of annihilating them. There was nothing glorious about Custer's last stand. But neither Whitman nor the nation could abide by such a truth. Cook-Lynn suggests that Whitman was motivated to write this poem not out of hatred of Native Americans, but because he saw the need to defend white culture. Thus the poem demonstrates how racism and religious prejudice serve not only to diminish Native American lives but also to project and protect white power and white privilege.

Historically Whites have often blamed Natives for the problems that befall them. Talk about the "Indian problem" is part of our national heritage. But what is thus described is not a Native American problem. It is a problem rooted in American Christianity. Therefore, it is crucial that we understand our theological heritage so that we do not mistakenly assume that racism or land hunger or greed alone explains the history of Native American genocide. As a practical matter, the settlers needed land. But their justification for taking the land and the lives of indigenous peoples was rooted at least partially in Christian theology.

Because the conquest of Native land and the subjugation of indigenous peoples remains an expression of Christianity, we must strive for a postcolonial Christianity. The word "postcolonial" does not suggest that colonialism has ended. Rather, postcolonial theory offers us a way to critique colonial Christianity. In the words of Kwok Pui-lan, "'Postcolonial imagination' refers to a desire, a determination, and a process of disengagement from the whole colonial syndrome."[15] Postcolonialism anticipates an alternative identity and a new mission for the mainline church.

Genocide

Since genocide means the deliberate and systematic destruction of a group or race, the charge of genocide carries with it moral culpability.[16] In what sense is the church guilty of seeking the deliberate destruction of Native American cultures and peoples? In what sense are white Christians guilty of Native genocide? To answer these questions we have to define carefully what the word "genocide" means.

The United Nations Genocide Convention defines genocide as "any of several kinds of acts committed with the intent to destroy, in whole or in part, a national, ethnic, racial or religious group as such."[17] Native scholar George Tinker, a member of the Osage Nation, defines genocide as, "[t]he effective destruction of a people by systematically or systemically (intentionally or unintentionally in order to achieve other goals) destroying, eroding, or undermining the integrity of the culture and system of values that defines a people and gives them life."[18] Elaborating on this definition, Tinker continues that genocide destroys a people's "sense of holistic and cultural integrity" and "effectively destroys a people by eroding both their self-esteem and the interrelationships that bind them together as a community."

Cook-Lynn defines genocide as the "systematic killing of people."[19] She says that it is *"always* premeditated, forethought, purposeful, designed." It does not *"just happen."* She identifies several types of genocide: *religious, racial* and *ethnic, political,* and *economic.* Each type of genocide has its own distinct motivating forces. Religious genocide, for example, may be fueled more by religious zeal than by theological reason. Racial and ethnic genocide may be rooted in historical cleavages that are linked with militaristic passion. Political and economic genocide may arise out of colonization, migration, and settling. Each type of genocide has its own unique lineage, but the types are not mutually exclusive. And they all share several traits in common. Cook-Lynn identifies a genocidal pattern that has four parts.

First, the perpetrators of genocide *pass laws* designed to prohibit certain types of behavior and to destroy others. Through this process, language, religious ceremonies, libraries, and other repositories of culture are targeted for destruction. Criminalizing the behavior of subjugated people also masks the genocidal intent of those who enact and enforce the laws. Second, the perpetrators of genocide *construct badges* that identify the victims of discrimination and further dehumanize them. Third, the perpetrators of genocide *concoct theories of conspiracy* that assist the general populace's ability to understand the supposed need to exploit or destroy the victims. Finally, the perpetrators of genocide build or *arrange appropriate centers for destruction,* annihilation, or subservience. Cook-Lynn points out that some people suggest that "reservations" for Native Americans were and are "extermination centers." Given this understanding of genocide, white Protestants are indeed complicit in Indian genocide.

No doubt labeling reservations as "extermination centers" strikes some white Christians as extreme. Yet it is not by accident that the following Native American reservations are located in six of the seven poorest counties in the nation: Crow Creek Indian Reservation (Buffalo County, SD), Pine Ridge Indian Reservation (Shannon County, SD), Cheyenne River Indian Reservation (Ziebach County, SD), Rosebud Reservation (Todd County, SD), and Standing Rock Reservation (Sioux County, ND and Corson County, SD).

The federal government is the "trustee" of these and all other reservations. The designation "reservation" means that the land is held in reserve for use by Native Americans. As trustee of these lands, the federal government voted to give itself plenary power. It controls and manages the use of these lands, with or without the consent of the people who live there. In addition, many essential reservation services are administered by federal agencies and depend on federal funds, which often are not reliable. For these reasons, Native American reservations are sometimes called "the ultimate welfare state."[20] George Tinker calls Native lands "national sacrifice areas."[21]

Still, the charge of genocide may seem unwarranted to some. The only recorded instance of a Christian minister engaged in the militaristic destruction of an indigenous community involves the Reverend John Chivington, who was known as the "fighting pastor." He was an ordained minister in the Methodist Church in Colorado. He was also a Colonel in the U.S. Army when he led an attack on a Cheyenne and Arapaho village at Sand Creek, Colorado, on November 29, 1864.

Colonel Chivington is quoted as saying in a Denver speech in August, 1864, "kill and scalp all, little and big...nits make lice."[22] A few months later he is said to have repeated this phrase as he led seven hundred cavalry troopers in an attack on a Cheyenne and Arapaho village at Sand Creek. It is impossible to know how many Native Americans died that day,[23] but we do know that Chivington's arsenal included four twelve-pound Mountain Howitzer guns plus the cavalry. In 2014, The United Methodist Church apologized for this attack and contributed $50,000 to a Sand Creek memorial.

Some members of the mainline church may contend that open warfare upon Native American peoples and communities is a thing of the past, and therefore the charge of genocide is without merit. Yet, as I shall document in the last two chapters of this book, the expropriation of Native lands, the desecration of sacred sites, and other public acts of aggression and neglect continue to take place on a fairly regular basis. Powerful commercial and political interests aligned against Native Americans thwart their drive to achieve self-governance. Cultural, economic, and religious genocide of Native peoples is still widely practiced in the United States today, often with little dissent from the majority culture or the church.

Deep Solidarity

"Deep solidarity" is a term coined by religious scholar Joerg Rieger to encourage people of faith to create new forms of unity that transcend diversities based on race, ethnicity, gender, sexuality, class, or other markers of differences.[24] Deep solidarity is based on a careful analysis of real life situations and finding in them common cause. Ethnic and cultural differences are respected. But rather than serving as a reason for division and noncooperation, the differences enhance our ability to work together to create alternative solutions to the situations in which we find ourselves—alternatives that benefit everyone. Deep solidarity between the mainline church and Native Americans is a pathway to interracial justice.

The concept of deep solidary expresses hope for a unity that will not be pulled apart by competing economic interests, disparate political priorities, conflicting cultural assumptions, or racial divides. Deep solidarity looks beyond what legal scholar Derrick Bell describes as a "theory of convergence,"[25] which is Bell's term for fleeting alliances formed across social and economic divides to further the self-interest of one party or the other—usually dictated by people in positions of power. Deep solidarity requires us to imagine new forms of social life, and to connect our imagination and our values with our deeds.

As Derrick Bell writes in *And We Are Not All Saved*, when there is a discrepancy between our deeply held beliefs and our daily behavior, when our beliefs and our behaviors do not align, when deep solidarity is not present, "We take refuge in the improbable and seek relief in increasingly empty repetitions of tarnished ideals."[26] This is a spiritual problem that often haunts the mainline church and informs our often expressed hope for reconciliation with Native Americans. We have a sincere hope, but our hope is not informed by careful analysis of the situation that can lead to deep solidarity.

The history of U.S. treaties with Native American nations illustrates our need for deep solidarity, if we are to strive for a more just society. There are eight hundred treaties between the United States and Native nations; the U.S. Senate has ratified 370 of them. Senator Daniel K. Inouye, who served as chairman of the Senate Select Committee on Indian Affairs, notes that the United States has violated provisions in every one of the ratified treaties.[27] Knowing this history lays a foundation for deep solidarity between the mainline church and tribal nations. As white Christians learn more about these treaties, they can advocate that the federal government honor them.

Deep solidarity calls for white Christians to learn a history that, frankly, most of us do not know. In addition, adopting the principle of deep solidarity entails a theological reformation. We white Christians have to replace binary theology that creates a sharply divided world: Christian/heathen, white/red, us/them. This binary lends itself to "*the idolatry of identity*"[28] and a toxic spirituality of fear. If we give "them" (the Native Americans) more land, self-governance, or more of anything else, then "we" (the whites) will have less. Thus, binary thinking precludes the possibility of deep solidarity. But what if binary thinking is an illusion in a multicultural world? What if the zero-sum trade-off (more for them means less for us) is a false way of thinking?

In his pioneering study *Orientalism*, Edward Said suggests that rather than thinking in binary terms of winners and losers, or allowing orthodoxy and dogma to rule, we need to recover a spirit of humanism that is "centered upon the agency of human individuality and subjective intuition, rather than received ideas and approved authority."[29] The study of human experience will be more fruitful if we use the norms of human freedom and knowledge. Said writes:

> Rather than the manufactured clash of civilizations, we need to concentrate on the slow working together of cultures that overlap, borrow from each other, and live together in far more interesting ways than any abridged or inauthentic mode of understanding can allow.[30]

The question that we must wrestle with in the postapology era is whether or not the mainline church can find more authentic and interesting ways of living in deep solidarity with Native peoples. N. Scott Momaday, a member of the Kiowa Tribe and a gifted poet and storyteller, pinpoints the struggle for white Christians in his essay "The Morality of Indian Hating." He writes, "The morality of intolerance has become in the twentieth century a morality of pity." He continues, "The contemporary white American is willing to assume responsibility for the Indian—he is willing to take on the burdens of oppressed people everywhere—but he is decidedly unwilling to divest himself of the false assumptions which impede his good intentions."[31] Instead of simply advocating *for* others, we must learn what it means to stand in deep solidarity *with* others. It is the only way to divest ourselves of our false assumptions.

NOTES

[1] Robert A. Williams, Jr., "Introduction," *Like a Loaded Weapon: The Rehnquist Court, Indian Rights, and the Legal History of Racism in America* (Minneapolis: University of Minnesota Press, 2005), xiii, xiv.

[2] Ibid., xiv.

[3]Beverly Daniel Tatum, *Why Are All the Black Kids Sitting Together in the Cafeteria?: And Other Conversations about Race* (New York: Basic Books, 1997), italics original, 7, 16 respectively.

[4]Paulo Freire, *Pedagogy of the Heart,* trans. Donaldo Macedo and Alexandre Oliveira (New York: The Continuum Publishing Company, 2000), italics original, 46, 104.

[5]Robert J. C. Young, *Postcolonialism: An Historical Introduction* (Oxford: Blackwell Publishing, 2001), identifies two types of colonialism: settlement and economic exploitive, and he distinguished colonialism from imperialism, 17.

[6]Eric K. Yamamoto, *Interracial Justice: Conflict & Reconciliation in Post-Civil Rights America* (New York: New York University Press, 1999).

[7]Ibid., italics original, 10, 11.

[8]Elizabeth Cook-Lynn, *Anti-Indianism in Modern America: a Voice from Tatekeya's Earth* (Urbana: University of Illinois Press, 2007), x.

[9]Ibid., 4.

[10]Andrea Smith, *Conquest: Sexual Violence and American Indian Genocide* (Cambridge, MA: South End Press, 2005), 9–10. Smith cites Andre Lopez, *Pagans in Our Midst* (Mohawk Nation: Awkesasne Notes, n.d.), fn. 10 on 193.

[11]Linguists debate when the word "squaw" was first used in a derogatory way. The word was not given inappropriate sexual connotations until perhaps the nineteenth century. In light of the controversy over the meaning of the word "squaw" since 1999 some states and tribes have taken steps to remove "squaw" from state sites or tribal locations.

[12]Smith, *Conquest,* 12.

[13]Whitman, "A Death Sonnet for Custer." This poem was later retitled "From Far Dakota's Cañons." *Leaves of Grass,* 404–5. See also, Cook-Lynn, *Anti-Indianism,* 6–9.

[14]Cook-Lynn, *Anti-Indianism,* 8. See also N. Scott Momaday, "The American West and the Burden of Belief," in *The Man Made of Words* (New York: St. Martin's Press, 1997), 89–107.

[15]Kwok Pui-lan, *Postcolonial Imagination & Feminist Theology* (Louisville: Westminster John Knox Press, 2005), 2–3. Pui-lan cites Ania Loomba, *Colonialism/Postcolonialism: The New Cultural Idiom* (London: Routledge, 1999), fn. 7 on 3.

[16]George E. Tinker, *Missionary Conquest: The Gospel and Native American Cultural Genocide* (Minneapolis: Fortress Press, 1993). Tinker quotes Jack Norton, *When Our Worlds Cried: Genocide in Northwestern California* (San Francisco: Indian Historian Press, 1979): "Genocide is a modern word for an old crime. It means the deliberate destruction of national, racial, religious or ethnic groups," 137. See fn. 9 on 126.

[17]United Nations, "Official Records of the Third Session of the General Assembly, Part I," Sixth Committee: Annexes to the Summary Records of Meetings, 1948, document A/C, 6/288 (Geneva) cited by Tinker, *Missionary Conquest,* 5, and fn. 11 on 127.

[18]Ibid., 6.

[19]Cook-Lynn, *Anti-Indianism,* italics original, 189–91, *passim.*

[20]Robert A. Williams Jr., *Like a Loaded Weapon: The Rehnquist Court, Indian Rights, and the Legal History of Racism in America* (Minneapolis: University of Minnesota Press, 2005), cites the Supreme Court's landmark decision in *Lone Wolf v. Hitchcock,* 187 U.S. 553 (1903), as the final consummation of the development of the congressional plenary power doctrine. In that case involving treaty rights of the confederated tribes of Kiowa, Comanches, and Apaches of Oklahoma, the Court held that Congress could unilaterally abrogate an Indian treaty under U.S. law, and there was nothing that the Supreme Court could do about it: Plenary authority over the tribal relations of the Indians has been exercised by Congress from the beginning, and the power has always been deemed a political one, not subject to be controlled by the judicial department of the government." The Court found that Congress has a moral obligation to act in good faith, but "The power exists to abrogate the provisions of an Indian treaty." See fn. 35 on 234–35.

[21]George Tinker, *American Indian Liberation: A Theology of Sovereignty*, (Maryknoll, NY: Orbis Books, 2008), 58. Tinker says the term was coined in a study commissioned by the National Academy of Science on resource development on Native lands. It was submitted to the Nixon administration in 1972 as input toward a national Native American policy, fn 5, 58.

[22]Manatka American Indian Council, "Chief Black Kettle: Presented by Dancing Eyes." Linda Wommack copyright 2000. All rights reserved. Reprinted under Fair Use doctrine of international copyright law. Full copyright retained by the original publication. www.manataka.org/page 161.html. http://www4.law.cornell.edu/uscode/17/107.html. Elsewhere the phrase, "nits make lice," is attributed to Chivington's superior officer, General Curtis, who had earlier ordered Chivington to "deliver up the Indians."

[23]Estimates of how many Native were murdered at Sand Creek range from a high of 1,600 (George Tinker, *American Indian Liberation*, 13) to a low estimate of 133 (Roxanne Dunbar-Ortiz, *An Indigenous Peoples' History of the United States* (Boston: Beacon Press, 2014), 137). Tinker cites Stan Hoig, *The Sand Creek Massacre* (Norman: University of Oklahoma Press, 1961). See fn 20 on 13. After the massacre, Chivington and his men desecrated the dead and carried severed body parts to Denver for display.

[24]Joerg Rieger and Kwok Pui-lan, *Occupy Religion: Theology of the Multitude* (Lanham, UK: Rowman & Littlefield, 2012), 18.

[25]For a discussion of Derrick Bell's "theory of convergence" and Robert Williams "singularity thesis," see Williams, *Loaded Weapon*," xxxiii-xxxvi. Williams cites Derrick Bell, "*Brown v. Board of Education* and the Interest Convergence Dilemma," *Harvard Law Review* 93 (1980): 524–25. See fn 60 on 210.

[26]Derrick Bell, *And We Are Not All Saved: The Elusive Quest for Racial Justice* (New York: Basic Books, 1987), 5.

[27]Daniel K. Inouye, "Preface," in *Exiled in the Land of the Free: Democracy, Indian Nations, and the U.S. Constitution*, Oren Lyons, John Mohawk, Vine Deloria, Jr., Laurence Hauptman, Howard Berman, Donald Grinde, Jr., Curtis Berkey, and Robert Venables, (Santa Fe, NM: Clear Light Publishers, 1992), x.

[28]Catherine Keller, Michael Nausner, and Mayra Rivera, eds., "Introduction," *Postcolonial Theologies: Divinity and Empire* (St. Louis: Chalice Press, 2004), italics original, 12.

[29]Edward W. Said, *Orientalism* (New York: Random House, Vintage Books Edition, 1979), xxix.

[30]Ibid.

[31]Momaday, "The Morality of Indian Hating," in *Man Made of Words*, 57–76, *passim* 69, 71–72.

PART TWO

Recognition

To overturn the colonial order that now oppresses and exploits Native Americans and undermines the witness of the church, we must identify and analyze the spiritual roots and political foundations of this order. This is the first step in the healing process.[1] The injustices Native Americans suffer were and are validated by operative social norms and collective representations that marginalize and denigrate them. Many of these norms and representations are grounded in Christian theology. We need to understand the circumstances, contexts and conflicts of the past to understand the present and promote healing for ourselves and for generations to come.

Recognition of the historical roots of anti-Native American attitudes is a way of reducing conflict and promoting "empathic justice." Critics of this type of justice contend that it undermines the impartial rule of law. I believe that empathy may help us recover the rule of law and motivate us to honor treaty obligations that have been ignored or neglected. From a theological perspective, empathetic justice is necessary if we are to obey the "royal law," which stipulates, "You shall love your neighbor as yourself" (Jas. 2:8).

Recognition not only puts us in touch with empathic justice, it also serves a sociological purpose. For example, understanding how the Crusades of the Middle Ages shaped Europe and established a Christian culture or knowing how the divine right of kings justified the Doctrine of Discovery allows us to address current controversies nondefensively. So informed, we can then begin to look for mutually beneficial ways to resolve present disputes.

Recognition also allows us to analyze the identity story adopted by the settlers, which Yamamoto calls the "stock story,"[2] and to understand its evolution. The settlers developed and used the biblical story of the Exodus to delineate their world, define their place in it, and denote their mission. N. Scott Momaday says these types of stories are not fact or fiction but "realities lived and believed. They are true."[3]

The biblical story of the Exodus was the primary identity story of the English settlers who came to Virginia and of those who came later to New England. Later, it influenced how the mainline church understood that its mission was to "civilize and Christianize Indians"—a mission for which it has apologized. In this postapology era we have to ask

26

ourselves if we still believe it. Is it true? What we want to know is how this narrative was constructed and used by our forebears so that we can evaluate it, modify it, or, more drastically, replace it with a new narrative that will allow us to live with respect for Native Americans without trying to impose uniformity.[4]

NOTES

[1]Eric Yamamoto discusses recognition as the first step leading toward healing in Eric K. Yamamoto, *Interracial Justice: Conflict & Reconciliation in Post-Civil Rights America* (New York: New York University Press, 1999), 175–85.

[2]"Stock story" is Eric Yamamoto's phrase. He defines these narratives as "stories groups themselves tell to explain the conflict and justify the group's response. Stock stories are "narratives shaped, told, and embraced by groups about themselves and others," 180.

[3]N. Scott Momaday, *The Man Made of Words* (New York: St. Martin's Press, 1997), 3.

[4]Jack Weatherford, *Savages and Civilizations: Who Will Survive?* (New York: Fawcett Columbine, 1994). Weatherford, an anthropologist, makes the point that with the emergence of a global culture, tribal and ethnic groups accentuate their differences. Cross-cultural contact can be a source of violence, but it may also foster cooperation, sharing, and mutual assistance. He warns: "Isolated populations without contact do not change; they stagnant and decline," 11. He concludes: "The challenge now facing us is to live in harmony without living in uniformity," 290.

3

The European Foundations of Cultural Imperialism

Identity stories rooted in religious beliefs and practices are always inescapably intertwined with other social and political institutions and events. To understand these stories and their context, there is no substitute for concrete historical examples. In this chapter we will examine seven episodes that prepared the way for the European, and most especially the English, invasion of what would become the United States of America. This examination is not an exhaustive analysis of a complex history, but rather an interpretive distillation of certain episodes that contribute to our understanding of Christian Anti-Native American praxis.

The events are separated by centuries, but together they create a pattern that reveals the interplay of religion, politics, and economics that became the basis for Christian anti–Native American attitudes. As we inquire into the significance of these events, we deepen our understanding of the present and become aware of untapped possibilities for a better future.

The First Crusade and the Doctrine of Discovery

Before the Crusades, Europe was a largely a land of independent kingdoms and principalities. A more unified Europe began to emerge after 1095, when Pope Urban II launched the First Crusade with a speech delivered at Clermont, France. In this speech, Urban cited the need of aiding Christians in the East, bemoaned the desecration of churches and holy places, affirmed the special sanctity of Jerusalem, promised both eternal and earthly rewards, and assured the assembled nobles and clergy that this cause was God's will and God's work.[1] Thousands of people, rich and poor alike, responded to the call.

Pope Urban II also issued the papal bull *Terra Nullius*. The meaning of this important document has evolved. Today, *Terra Nullius* is a principle of international law. As such it refers to "nobody's land," meaning land that was never the territory of a sovereign state. In the eleventh century *Terra Nullius* meant "empty land," or "uninhabited land." It was land where "heathens"—people without souls and incapable of faith—lived. This papal edict gave Christians the right to invade the Holy Lands and wage war on Muslims. By the seventeenth century *Terra Nullius* also meant "uncultivated land"—meaning land where the habitants had no permanent settlements but, in the words of Puritan preachers, "roamed up and down like wild beasts." Therefore, the land that the Europeans "discovered" was uninhabited. *Terra Nullius* and later papal bulls became the foundation for the Doctrine of Discovery.

By the end of the crusading movement in 1291, European Christendom was acclimated to going to war against non-Christians. When European explorers came to the Americas centuries later, they convinced themselves that they had discovered a land inhabited by primitive peoples who lacked both religion and civilization.

Infidels and Indians

A second manifestation of Western Christendom's ideology occurred in Florence, Italy, in 1366. Fourteenth-century Florence was the center of the Italian Renaissance and a commercial hub.[2] It was not yet a secular city, but it was no longer dominated by the church. A recovery of Greek and Roman classics infused Christian piety with a spirit of humanism that tempered rigid theological doctrine and dogma and curtailed the power of the church. The Priors of Florence (the city council) had to find ways to blend the needs created by the vibrant economy and the changing cultural milieu of the city with the teachings of the church, which was still a potent force. The redefinition of the meaning of "infidel" illustrates how they fit together established religious teachings and the needs of a changing society.

To meet the labor demands of the burgeoning economy, Florentine leaders of business and commerce were importing women from countries dominated by the Eastern Orthodox Church to work in Italian factories and to be household servants.[3] The practice of human trafficking solved the labor problem, but it was an unsavory business that offended basic morality. So in 1366 the Priors of Florence declared that people not born of Latin Christian parents were and would forever remain irredeemable "infidels," thereby giving the practice of human trafficking religious sanction and absolving faithful Italians of any guilt associated with it.

Laura E. Donaldson, a Cherokee and Scots-Irish scholar, says that this new definition of "infidel" contributed to a religious paradigm that made Christianity a powerful tool of conquest in the Americas because it fed into "an evolving context of discrimination that nurtured the notion of non-Europeans as separate, distinct, and inferior 'races.'"[4] Donaldson argues that "this semantic and theological redefinition of the infidel also influenced the belief that God created American Indians for the specific purpose of becoming slaves to European Christians."[5] Elsewhere Donaldson writes: "Until all peoples grasp the intricate relationships binding colonialism, gender and religion together, all dreams of a genuinely new world order will remain only the shadow of an ideal."[6]

Romanus Pontifex and Inter Caetera

The papal bull *Romanus Pontifex* that Pope Nicholas V issued in 1454 at the beginning of the European Age of Discovery and Conquest granted Portugal's King Alfonzo V the authority to "invade, search out, capture, vanquish, and subdue all Saracens and pagans whatsoever, and other enemies of Christ wheresoever placed, and the kingdoms, dukedoms, principalities, dominions, possessions, and all other movable and immovable goods whatsoever held and possessed by them and to reduce their persons to perpetual slavery."[7]

Four decades later in 1493, Pope Alexander VI issued a new papal bull, *Inter Caetera*, in which he gave the Spanish crown of Castile and Aragon similar rights to conquer "barbarous nations" and spread the Catholic faith so "that the health of the soul be cared for."[8]

By issuing the second bull, the pope established himself as the mediator of political disputes between European sovereigns. But he did much more than that. Vine Deloria, Jr., whom George Tinker calls "the late dean of American Indian academics,"[9] contends that "the Christian church saw a means of directing the invasion of new lands by placing its imprimatur on exploitation in effect taking a percentage of the loot in return for blessing the enterprise."[10] More generally, *Inter Caetera* spelled out in clear terms the Christian attitude toward the world. As Deloria notes: "Plainly the pope was supervising not the divinely ordained division of the world's land but national hunting licenses for rape and pillage."[11] Deloria contends that the pope bestowed upon Christian rulers the right to conquer foreign lands and to exploit and if need be annihilate the people who lived there without apology.

Sublimis Dei

The papal bull *Sublimis Dei*, issued by Pope Paul III on May 29, 1537, softened the theology of conquest, but did not essentially alter it. The pope did not discourage the subjugation of indigenous peoples or their conversion to Christianity, but he did advocate for their humanity. The topic of this encyclical was "the enslavement and evangelization of Indians." It declared: "All men have the faculties to receive faith" and "The Indians are truly men and…they…are not only capable of understanding the Catholic Faith but, according to our information, they desire exceedingly to receive it." He went on to stipulate that "said Indians and all other people who may later be discovered by Christians, are by no means to be deprived of their liberty or the possession of their property, even though they be outside the faith of Jesus Christ." He also specifically forbade enslavement: "Indians and other people should be converted to the faith of Jesus Christ by preaching the word of God and by the example of good and holy living."[12]

The encyclical *Sublimis Dei* was influenced by the work and witness of Bartolomé de las Casas, a Dominican friar who came to the Americas in 1515. Las Casas was officially appointed "Protector of the Indians," an administrative office charged with looking after the welfare of Native peoples. In 1543, he became the first bishop of Chiapas, Mexico. Las Casas argued that the policy of the crown and the church should be to convert indigenous peoples to Christianity, not to enslave them or to kill them. His influential book, *A Short Account of the Destruction of the Indies*, published in 1542, was well known in Europe.[13]

The poet John Donne, who was the Dean of St. Paul's Cathedral in London from 1621 to 1631 and a strong advocate for the Jamestown colony, knew the work of Las Casas and perhaps saw himself in this tradition when he declared that Jamestown was a "holy experiment" established for the purpose of converting Native Americans to Christianity.

The English Reformation and Counter-Reformation

The causes of the English Reformation were rooted more deeply in politics and economics than in theology. Tax policy, indulgences, investiture debates, and the crown's need for funds figured prominently in the long-running dispute between King Henry VIII and the pope. Also, Henry's, insistence that the pope annul his marriage to Catherine of Aragon so that he would be free to marry Anne Boleyn and the pope's refusal to comply with his royal demand turned the long simmering feud between the crown and the church into an open split. By 1542, following the dissolution of the monasteries, Henry had centralized power in the hands of the state. When Henry died, the King of England was the Head of the Church of England, and England was no longer part of Roman Catholic Christendom.

Mary Tudor, Henry's daughter and his successor to the throne, was a devout Roman Catholic.[14] She was determined to repair the breach with the papacy and return England to the fold of Catholic Christendom. But Mary ruled over a divided realm. When recalcitrant Protestants refused to abandon the Church of England, Mary instituted heresy trials, which began on January 22, 1555.

The Marian Persecutions lasted for three bloody years but only succeeded in convincing dissident evangelicals that suffering was the mark of the true church and in confirming their belief that the pope was the Antichrist. In John Foxe's *Acts and Monuments of these latter and perilous days touching on matters of the Church*, otherwise known as Foxe's *Book of Martyrs*, the faithful read an account of their part in God's plan.

The publication became a bestselling book in Elizabethan England, second only to the Bible. Much more than a record of persecution, Foxe's book, according to historian Paul Johnson, "embodied the English national-religious myth, which had been growing in power in the later Middle Ages and came to maturity during the Reformation decades—the myth that the English had replaced the Jews as the Elect Nation, and were divinely appointed to do God's will on earth."[15] The destruction of the Spanish Armada in 1588 and the growth of England's navy and sea power during the reigns of Henry VIII and Elizabeth I reinforced England's belief in this myth. England was on its way to becoming a global power with a divine mandate when Elizabeth ascended to the throne.

The English Invasion of Ireland

When Mary's Protestant half-sister Elizabeth became Queen Elizabeth I, English citizens loyal to papal authority called her the "bastard queen," because the Roman Catholic Church had never recognized Henry's divorce from Catherine of Aragon or his marriage to Anne Boleyn, Elizabeth's mother. Plots to replace Elizabeth with an heir to the throne whom Catholics considered more legitimate were presented to the pope at various times during Elizabeth's reign, and as a result she was always wary of the intentions of the pope and of Catholic Spain. This atmosphere of distrust served as the backdrop to the English invasion of America.

During Elizabeth's reign, the long-simmering tensions between the English and the Irish were inflamed by a group known as the "West Country men," who later figured prominently in the English invasion of America. Their company included Sir Richard Grenville, Sir John Hawkins, Sir Walter Raleigh, Sir Humphrey Gilbert, Baron De La Warr, John Mason, and others. Their avowed purpose was to: "1. To plant the Christian religion. 2. To trafficke. 3. To conquer."[16]

Meanwhile, during the Nine Years War, 1594–1603, the English employed a scorched earth policy to demoralize and punish the rebellious Irish. The policy transformed vast areas of Ireland into waste lands. As much as a third of the population of Ireland died of famine. The confiscated land was then turned into English plantations. As historian Alan Taylor explains in *American Colonies*, the English brought the lessons they learned about using this plantation policy to conquer and colonize the Irish with them to America:

> In Ireland, the English developed both the techniques and the rhetoric of colonial conquest. In Ireland, the English learned to consider resisting peoples as dirty, lazy, treacherous, murderous, and pagan savages, little better than wild animals, and to treat them accordingly. In Virginia, the English employed the same language and meted out the same treatment whenever Indians

violated the initial role cast for them: grateful innocents eager to submit to their superior benefactors.[17]

The Pauperization of Elizabethan England

England's colonization of North America was fueled by the English Reformation and Counter-Reformation, and honed by the war with the Irish. The success of England's imperial ambition was ensured by the pauperization of its masses. At one time, perhaps eighty percent of the population of Tudor England lived in rural areas. Peasants and tillers of the land shared the agricultural commons. The nobility's enclosure of these commons with walls and fences and moats turned this shared agricultural land into private estates and turned rural peasants into the landless urban poor.

In order to control the swelling ranks of idle persons, beggars, and vagabonds, Parliament enacted a series of Poor Laws, which criminalized poverty and made England the first modern welfare state. Sanctioned by the new laws, the state rather than the church administered programs to care for the poor. However, whereas the church's purpose had been to alleviate the plight of the poor, the crown's interest was in controlling the poor and maintaining order.[18]

The Beggars Act of 1597 was emblematic of the state's policy. Under this law, vagrancy and beggary became crimes punishable by public flogging until the blood ran, imprisonment, deportation, and execution. Many vagrants and beggars were conscripted into the Royal Navy, while others were sent overseas as indentured servants to supply labor for England's colonies, often called "prisons without walls." Sir John Popham, Chief Justice of the King's Bench from 1592 to 1607 and one of the leading organizers of the Virginia Company, convicted many "sturdy rogues and beggars" of violating the Beggars Act of 1597 and sent them into exile.[19]

As Chief Justice of the King's Bench, Sir Edward Coke continued the policies of Popham. Robert Williams argues that Coke's decision "in *Calvin's Case* (1608) suggests a more thorough absorption of the medieval Christian crusading tradition and its highly negative view on pagan and infidel rights into England's common law tradition."[20] Coke stated that the law regarded infidels as "perpetual enemies (*perpetui inimici*) of a Christian kingdom."[21] As a result of this decision, the infidels had no rights under English common law. They were enemies of Christ and, therefore, also enemies of the state. The ruling had both domestic and international consequences. Once an infidel kingdom was subjugated by a Christian ruler, the laws of the infidel were abrogated.

The first known felon convicted under the Beggars Act and sent to Virginia arrived in 1607. During the first half of the seventeenth century, labor-market entrepreneurs plucked up the poor and shipped them initially to Virginia and later to New England.[22] In 1619, the Virginia

Company contracted with the city of London to ship several hundred poor children between the ages of eight and sixteen from the city's Bridewell Prison to America.[23] In 1627 alone, between 1,400 and 1,500 children were shipped from England's "houses of sorrow" to Virginia.[24]

Leading clerics like John Donne supported the deportation policy. As late as 1622, Donne preached a sermon to the Honorable Company of the Virginia Plantation in which he assured his audience that the Virginia Company "shall sweep your streets, and wash your dores, from idle persons, and the children of idle persons, and employ them; and truly, if the whole Countrey were such a Bridewell, to force idle persons to work, it had a good use."[25] Donne and many others "wanted √America to *function* as a prison."[26] Thus the pauperization of England had a direct bearing on the colonization of North America. The sheer number of people sent to Jamestown eventually overwhelmed the Powhatan population living in the James River Valley.

NOTES

[1]Dana Carleton Munro, "The Speech of Pope Urban II at Clermont, 1095," *The American Historical Review*, vol. 11, no. 2 (Jan. 1906), 231–42. Published by Oxford University Press on behalf of the American Historical Association. http://www.jstor.org/stable/1834642?seq=12#page_scan_tab_contents Accessed 12/14/2015.

[2]Sir Peter Hall, "The Rediscovery of Life: Florence 1400–1500," *Cities in Civilization* (New York: Pantheon Books, 1998), 69–113.

[3]Paola Pinelli, "From Dubrovnik (Ragusa) to Florence: Observations on the Recruiting of Domestic Servants in the Fifteenth Century," *The Medievalists.net*, January 1, 2011. www.medievalists.net/2011/01/01/from-dubrovnik-to-florence-recruitment-of-servants-in-fifteenth-century/. Accessed 5/15/2012.

[4]"The Breasts of Columbus: A Political Anatomy of Postcolonialism and Feminist Religious Discourse," in *Postcolonialism, Feminism & Religious Discourse*, ed. Laura E. Donaldson and Kwok Pui-lan (New York: Routledge, 2002), 41–61, 44. Donaldson cites David Stannard, *American Holocaust: The Conquest of the New World* (New York: Oxford University Press, 1992), 209. See fn 13 on 59.

[5]Ibid.

[6]Donaldson, "God, Gold and Gender," in Donaldson and Pui-lan, *Postcolonialism*, 5–14, 6.

[7]Nicholas V, *Romanus Pontifex*, January 8, 1455. http://www.nativeweb.org/pages/legal/indig-romanus-pontifex.html. Accessed 6/25/2014. The translation on this site is reproduced, as published in Francis Gardener Davenport, ed., *European Treaties bearing on the History of the United States and its Dependencies to 1648*, Carnegie Institute of Washington, 1917, Washington, D.C., 20–26. The original text in Latin is in the same volume, 13–20.

[8]Pope Alexander VI, *Inter Caetera*, May 4, 1493. http://www.nativeweb.org/pages/legal/indig-inter-caetera.html. Accessed 7/8/2014. The translation of this text is reproduced in Davenport, ed., *European Treaties*, 75–78. The original Latin text is found in the same volume, 72–75.

[9]George Tinker, *American Indian Liberation: A Theology of Sovereignty*, (Maryknoll, NY: Orbis Books, 2008), 71.

[10]Vine Deloria, Jr., *God is Red: A Native View of Religion* (Golden, CO: Fulcrum Publishing, 2003), 30th Anniversary Edition, 258. Since 1972, when Deloria first called attention to *Inter Caetera*, native groups have been calling on the Vatican to revoke this bull. For a listing of actions by native peoples from 1972 to 1988 see "Timeline of the Effort by Indigenous Nations and People Calling upon the Vatican to Revoke *Inter Caetera*." http://www.nativevillage.org/International%20Council%20of%2013%20 INDIGENOUS%20GR/GR%20Other%20pages/timeline. Accessed 7/8/2014.

[11]Ibid., 259.

[12]Pope Paul III, "*Sublimus Dei,*" *Papal Encyclicals Online.* http://www.papalencyclicals. net/Paul03/p3subli.htm. Accessed 5/14/2014.

[13]For a summary of Las Casas' influence see Robert J. C. Young, *Postcolonialism: An Historical Introduction* (Oxford: Blackwell Publishing, 2001), 75–76. See also Hjamil A. Martinez-Vázques, "Bartolomé de Las Casas," in *Empire and the Christian Tradition*, ed. Pui-lan, Compier, and Rieger, 201–14. John C. Mohawk, "Indians and Democracy: No One Ever Told Us," *Exiled in the Land of the Free*, 43–71.

[14]Susan Ronald, *Heretic Queen: Queen Elizabeth I and the Wars of Religion* (New York: St. Martin's Press, 2012).

[15]Paul Johnson, *A History of the American People* (New York: HarperCollins Publishers, 1997), 19–20. Johnson writes with an appreciation of the contribution of Christianity to English settlement and westward expansion. His views on the Native Americans are less so. He asserts that there was "no lack of sympathy" on the white side. "The real problem of the Indians, in confronting the whites, and especially their government, was the absence of leaders who knew how to manipulate the Washington system." He describes the Dawes Act as a "retreat from the reservation policy." The choice Native Americans face was and is "to be preserved in amber as tribal societies" or assimilation, 521.

[16]Alan Taylor, *American Colonies* (New York: Viking, 2001), 119.

[17]Ibid., 123.

[18]Frances Fox Piven and Richard Cloward, "Chapter One: Relief, Labor, and Civil Disorder: An Overview," *Regulating the Poor: The Functions of Public Welfare* (New York: Random House, Inc., 1971), 3–42.

[19]Peter Linebaugh and Marcus Rediker, *The Many-Headed Hydra: Sailors, Slaves, Commoners, and the Hidden History of the Revolutionary Atlantic*, reprint ed. (Boston: Beacon Press, 2013), 19–20, 49–60.

[20]Robert A. Williams, Jr., *Savage Anxieties: The Invention of Western Civilization* (New York: Palgrave Macmillan, 2012), italics original, 189.

[21]Ibid., italics original, 189. *Calvin's Case*, 77, Eng. Rep. 377, 378 (1608), fn 25 on 245.

[22]Linebaugh and Rediker, *Many-Headed Hydra*, suggest that this is the historic base on which American slavery was founded, 58. They cite Eric Williams, *Capitalism and Slavery* (New York: Capricorn Books, 1966), 19. See fn 33 on 363.

[23]Bridewell Palace was built as a residence for King Henry VIII. His son, King Edward VI gave it to the City of London for use as an orphanage and a correction house for women. It was both a prison and a hospital.

[24]Linebaugh and Rediker, *Many-Headed Hydra*, 59. Linebaugh and Rediker cite Robert C. Johnson, "The Transportation of Vagrant Children from London to Virginia, 1618–1622" in Howard R. Reinmuth, ed., *Early Stuart Studies: Essays in Honor of David Harris Williams* (Minneapolis: University of Minnesota Press, 1970), 137–51; Walter Hart Blumenthal, *Brides from Bridewell: Female Felons Sent to Colonial America* (Rutland, VT: Charles E. Tuttle Co., 1962), 65, 105, 107.

[25]Ibid., 59. Linebaugh and Rediker cite John Donne, "A Sermon Preached to the Honorable Company of the Virginian Plantation," in *The Sermons of John Donne*, ed. George R. Porter and Evelyn M. Simpson (Berkeley: University of California Press, 1959), 4:272. See fn 35 on 363.

[26]Ibid., italics original, 59.

4

Coming to America

Protestant Christianity came to the shores of Virginia in the context of English imperialism, "the policy of extending the rule of empire over colonies for the reason of conquest and profit."[1] Shifts in agriculture, an increase of wage labor, growth of urban populations, the pauperization peasants, and the expansion of world trade enabled the establishment of Jamestown, the spearhead of English colonization in America. While financial gain was a primary motive for investors and speculators, cultural imperialism was very much on the mind of some of the English who championed the Jamestown colony, and those who later came to New England. To tell their story I have divided this chapter into four parts. The first part gives an account of the founding of Jamestown. The second focuses on those settlers who created a Bible commonwealth in New England. The third discusses the Pequot War, praying towns, and cultural genocide. The chapter concludes with Increase Mather's interpretation of King Phillip's War. I believe that in an indirect way this war and Mather's interpretation of it prepared the hearts and minds of the faithful for the Great Awakening, a topic discussed in the next chapter.

Jamestown: The Holy Experiment

The Church of England contributed to both the financial support and the spiritual legitimation of the Jamestown Colony. The third paragraph of the First Charter of the Virginia Company is a testament to the important role of religion in the founding of the colony. It reads:

> We, greatly commending, and graciously accepting of, their Desires for the Furtherance of so noble a Work, which may, by the Providence of Almighty God, hereafter tend to the Glory of his Divine Majesty, in propagating of Christian Religion to such People, as yet live in Darkness and miserable Ignorance of the true Knowledge and Worship of God, and may in time bring the Infidels and Savages, living in those parts, to human Civility, and to a settled and quiet Government: DO, by these our Letters Patents, graciously accept of, and agree to, their humble and well-intended Desires.[2]

The inclusion of this article in the Charter was more than a pious formality. When the charter company was having difficulty raising sufficient funds to underwrite the colony by appealing solely to the pecuniary interests of potential investors, leading clergy reminded the faithful of their obligation to spread the Protestant message. Church leaders assured their flock that the "Angel of Virginia" was calling the faithful to come to the New World, just as the "Angel of Macedonia" had once summoned Paul (Acts 16:9).[3]

The first Protestant church in the "New World" was established in Virginia. The Reverend Robert Hunt was the first spiritual advisor and pastor of the colony. R. S. Thomas, the official historiographer of the Diocese of Southern Virginia in the late nineteenth century, reports in his address to the Sixth Annual Council of the Diocese of Southern Virginia, entitled "The Religious Element in the Settlement at Jamestown," that daily Common Prayer was performed every morning and evening, that there were two sermons on Sunday, and that Holy Communion was celebrated every three months.[4] Thomas also notes: "Not only the charters, but every paper, ever published by, or for, the London Company contained the strongest appeals to the religious sentiments of the people."[5] He adds: "The eyes of all Europe are looking upon our endeavors to spread the Gospell among the Heathen people of Virginia; to plant our English nation there; and to settle at in those parts which may be peculiar to our nation, so that, we may, thereby, be secured from being eaten out of all profits of trade by our industrious neighbors."[6] Lastly, Thomas reminds his audience that it was the marriage of Pocahontas, or Matoa, the daughter of Powhatan, to John Rolfe in 1614 that helped bring an end to the first Anglo-Powhatan War.

Woefully unprepared for the life that awaited them in America, only thirty-eight members of the initial Jamestown party of 104 were still alive nine months after their arrival. So the Virginia Company sent more settlers. By December of 1609, Jamestown had 202 residents. However, by the following spring, only sixty remained alive. Still, more settlers were to come.

Members of the Powhatan Confederation who lived in the James River Valley could not possibly have anticipated that ten thousand English settlers would come to Jamestown between 1607 and 1622.[7] The sheer number of English settlers ensured the success of the Jamestown Colony, but not the success of the Holy Experiment.

The Powhatan response to the presence of the Virginians was guided by a policy of prudent hospitality. They brought the settlers food and taught them survival skills. At the same time, they did not want to be overrun by the English. Therefore, the Powhatan adopted a containment policy designed to prevent the establishment of new settlements. This policy hampered the efforts of the Virginians to relocate to more favorable surroundings, and worsened the deadly consequences of outbreaks of disease.

As anthropologist Helen C. Rountree, a leading researcher and writer on Virginia tribes, documents in her study "Powhatan Priests and English Rectors: World Views and Congregations in Conflict," cultural differences sharpened the economic and political competition already going on.[8]

According to Rountree, the English way was characterized by monotheism, patriarchy, and order. God the Father was the supreme ruler. Family life and society were structured hierarchically and patriarchally. Men were head of the family and political leaders. They took for granted that land was a commodity to be subdued and used to produce food. As the Israelites had been given the task of taking Canaan and using it for God's glory, so the Jamestown settlers assumed that they were given the task of taking and transforming the "New World." Churches were built in designated places for religious rituals focused on life and death and presided over by male clergy who believed that human nature was sinful and that it was their divine mission to convert the non-Christian Natives to their faith.

In stark contrast, she writes, Powhatan religion and life revolved around horticulture, the Chesapeake Bay, and the weather. Their society was communitarian, egalitarian, and democratic. They had no private property, no master, and no king. Community life was organized so that every family had access to water, farmland, and forest—the essentials of life. No one was starving. Both women and men were chiefs. Leadership positions were passed on matrilineally. Corporal punishment was not used. Rather than adopting the settler's goal of trying to tame an unruly world, the Powhatan understood their place in a sacred and life-sustaining world.

The ethnocentric Europeans and arguably equally ethnocentric Powhatan were poorly prepared to understand much less accept the spiritual convictions and cultural ways of the other. However, Linebaugh and Rediker tell us that the Powhatan way of life and their hospitality persuaded one in seven English Virginians to desert Jamestown and become "Anglo-Powhatans" during the winter of 1609–1610.[9] These desertions prompted the *Laws Divine, Moral, and Martial*, sanctioned by the Second Charter of Virginia (1609).[10] This document transferred governance of the colony to the Governor of Jamestown and his advisory council, established martial law, and granted the colony favorable tax and trade policies. Lord De La Warr, an important investor in the colony and a seasoned soldier with experience in the Irish campaign, was appointed the first governor of Jamestown under the new Charter.

Kirkpatrick Sale writes in *The Conquest of Paradise* that after De La Warr arrived, Jamestown was "the equivalent of a military invasion force in a foreign land."[11] Settlers who ran away to the Native Americans were retaken by military expeditions and brought back to Jamestown for punishment. Some of these prisoners were hanged, others burned or shot, while still others were tied to trees and left to starve to death.[12] When De La Warr was forced to return to London for reasons of health, the new governor, Thomas Dale, perpetuated this reign of terror.

Both Governor De La Warr and Governor Dale were determined to expand into the James River Valley. This determination precipitated the first Anglo-Powhatan War, which began in 1610 when De La Warr sent a detachment of seventy men to attack the Paspahegh capital. The soldiers burned down the houses, destroyed the corn fields, and kidnapped a Powhatan queen and her children, all of whom they subsequently murdered. Such total warfare was new to the Native Americans.

The steady supply of people coming from England and the settler's aggressive policies enabled Dale to successfully establish the city of Hericus in 1611. Two years later, Alexander Whitaker, a minister in Henrico (Hericus), wrote a tract in which he described the Indians of the Tidewater region as "naked slaves of the divell,"[13] who presumably needed to be saved. In 1618 the colony received a royal charter for the proposed University of Henrico. In 1622 they established a school for Native Americans with the intention of civilizing the savages and bringing the heathen into the Christian fold.

In the beginning the Virginia Company of London expected to find gold and silver in the New World. But this plan for wealth was abandoned in 1614 when John Rolfe cultivated a tobacco product that could compete with Spanish tobacco in the British market. The financial success of tobacco spurred new interest in the colony and made it less dependent on the good will of the Powhatans. Soon tobacco plantations lined the James River Valley.

The Powhatan responded to this new situation by adopting an ever more aggressive containment policy. Taking bold action, on March 22, 1622 the Powhatan launched a surprise attack on the tobacco plantations and killed 347 men, women, and children, approximately twenty percent of the population. Mistakenly, they thought that they had taught the settlers a lesson about the necessity of respecting boundaries.

It took time for news of the attack to reach London, where, on July 3, 1622, John Donne had finally realized his long cherished hope of becoming an honorary member of the Virginia Company Council. Within a week of his election, word of the "bloody massacre" reached England. In a sermon preached before the Virginia Company on November 13, 1622, Donne counseled calm, and held out hope for the future conversion of the Native Americans.[14]

But Edward Waterhouse, secretary of the Virginia Company, saw the "bloody massacre" as an opportunity to rid the colony of Powhatans, whom he called a "perfidious and inhumane people."[15] He labeled them "this viperous brood." Waterhouse urged that Virginians "with a clear conscience follow the easier and more profitable way of conquering the Indians, seizing their land, and compelling them to servitude and drudgery." "Victory may be gained many ways," he said, "by force, by surprise, by famine, by burning their corn, burning and destroying their canoes, and houses, by breaking their fishing wares...by pursuing and chasing them with our horses and blood-hounds."[16] Waterhouse wanted the Virginians to annihilate the Powhatan Confederacy.

Frederick Fausz, a leading historian of the "Bloody Massacre," calls it the "Powhatan Uprising."[17] The fact that the Powhatan did not kill all the settlers leads him to conclude that they did not want to annihilate the English; they only wanted them to stay in their place. The attack was consistent with their containment policy.

The Uprising and the response of the Virginia Company brought an end to the "Holy Experiment." Frederick Fausz believes this rupture between the church and the Virginia Company was a watershed event. Once the London clergy withdrew their support, the colonists and their financial backers accelerated the evolution of the colony from a holy experiment to a commercial plantation of tobacco farmers. Fausz concludes: "By 1625, the Virginia-English had discarded ideology and discovered...personal reasons for coming to and staying in the New World. Such goals would later be rediscovered in colony after colony, and the net effect in every case would be uniformly negative and tragic for the Indians."[18]

The Bible Commonwealth[19]

The Pilgrims arrived on the south shore of Massachusetts Bay in 1620 to establish Plymouth Colony. Ten years later, approximately 1,500 Puritans were added to their number, and during the Great Migration of the 1630s, another 14,000. While the Pilgrims and the Puritans have distinct histories, they shared a common belief in the kingdom of God, which, as H. Richard Niebuhr explains, was not "something to be built" but "a rule to be obeyed."[20] A positive allegiance to the government of God united the Puritans and Pilgrims. In New England as in Virginia, the sheer number of settlers who came to the colonies simply overwhelmed the indigenous population.

In 1650, Massachusetts had one minister for every 415 persons, compared to one minister for every 3,239 persons in Virginia. By law, every town in New England had a church, and every church was supported by taxes. All the inhabitants had to attend midweek lectures and Sunday services, which were morning and afternoon. Devout Puritans believed that they were heirs to Israel's covenant with God, and they were intent on building a godly society. Hardships and setbacks they understood to be chastening rods that called for individual soul-searching, collective reassessment, and renewed dedication.

Governor William Bradford's *History of Plimoth Plantation* illustrates how Protestant theology shaped the New England way. After explaining that the Pilgrims had to leave Holland "for sundry weighty and solid reasons," Bradford describes New England as "those vast and unpeopled countries of America, which are frutfull and fitt for habitation, being devoyd of all civill inhabitants, wherther are only salvage and brutish men, which range up and downe, litle otherwise then the wild beasts of the same."[21] "But," he continues, "their condition was not ordinarie; their ends were good and honourable; their calling lawfull, and urgente; and therfore they might expecte the blessing of God in their proceding. Yea, though they should loose their lives in this action, yet might they have comforte in the same, and their endeavors would be honourable."

Governor Bradford's portrayal of Native Americans was disingenuous at best, for the Plymouth colony entered their first treaty with Pokanokets in 1621. George Tinker reports that the colony lost half its number to starvation and disease. They were "in a position of pronounced weakness when the Pokanokets approached them entreating an alliance." In spite of their weakness, "the colonists chose to interpret the treaty as one in which the Pokanoket nation became subjugated to the superior English."[22] In contrast, the Pokanokets thought they were establishing kinship bonds.

As in Jamestown, the cultural divide between the two communities contributed to misunderstanding and conflict. To impress upon the natives the superiority of white culture, Captain Miles Standish led a small military force in a preemptive assassination attack against a number of Massachusett Tribe leaders in 1623. Tinker reports: "To complete the reign of terror, the head of one of the sachem was impaled on a post outside the fortification of Plymouth as a warning to other Indians."[23]

Massachusetts Bay Colony's expanding population and economic success brought them into conflict with other settlers and with the region's tribes, most especially the Pequot Tribe that lived in the lower portion of the Connecticut River Valley. The Pequots' economic interests rivaled those of the Puritans. In addition there was competition and conflict between the Pequots and other tribes in the area, notably the Uncas, the Mohegans, and the Narragansetts. The Puritans were able to take advantage of these rivalries as they sought to establish their own supremacy, but first they had to establish order within the colony.

The Antinomian Controversy, also known as the Free Grace Controversy, threatened the Puritan's religious experiment in New

England. The controversy, which began in 1636, pitted magistrates and leading members of the colony's clergy against a dissident group led by the Reverend John Cotton and, most notably, Anne Hutchinson. The controversy ended when John Winthrop won the gubernatorial race in 1637 and the Boston magistrates who supported Hutchinson were voted out of office. Thereafter, Massachusetts was committed to a policy of strict religious orthodoxy and conformity. Hutchinson was banished from the colony in 1637 and then excommunicated in 1638, which, Linebaugh and Rediker tell us, "removed opposition to the Pequot War and cleared the way for slavery."[24]

The Pequot War

The Puritans lived in an uneasy truce with the Pequot Indians in what is now southern Connecticut and Rhode Island. The murder of a white trader and Native-kidnapper, John Oldham, provided the excuse for going to war. Captain John Mason and Captain John Underhill, both veterans of the English war upon the Irish, led the campaign. Mason's account is found in *An Epitome or Brief History of the Pequot War*.[25] The following material is based on Mason's *Brief History*.

Captain Mason and Captain Underhill led ninety well-armed soldiers into battle in early May, 1637. They attacked a Pequot encampment of six or seven hundred men, women, and children on the banks of the Mystic River and set it ablaze. Most of the Pequot died in the inferno. Those who escaped the consuming fire were either shot or bayonetted by the soldiers. According to Mason's count roughly one hundred and fifty warriors died in the fire; the rest were women, children, and old men. Only seven Pequot were taken captive, and about seven escaped. Mason and Underhill went on to lead two more campaigns against the Pequot after the raid at Mystic River. They succeeded in almost extinguishing the tribe.

When the Treaty of Hartford brought the war to an end in 1638, the victorious settlers took possession of all the Pequot land and made it a crime to speak the Pequot language or even mention their name. The few surviving members of the tribe were either sold into slavery or kept as domestic servants in Puritan homes. Historian Nathaniel Philbrick has observed that "with the Pequot War, New England was introduced to the horrors of European-style genocide."[26]

Praying Towns and Cultural Genocide

The Reverend John Eliot arrived in Roxbury, Massachusetts, in 1631, to begin his ministry as the pastor of the Roxbury congregation. It was a position he held for the next forty years. He had a deep interest in the Native Americans and became an energetic evangelist to them. For this reason he is known as the "Apostle to the Indians."

The 1628 charter of the colony pledged that the inhabitants "maie be soe religiously, peaceablie, and civilly governed, as their good Life and orderlie Conversation, maie wynn and incite the Natives of Country, to the Knowledg and Obedience of the onlie true God and Savior of Mankinde, and the Christian Fayth, which in our Royall Intention, and the Adventurers free Profession, is the principall Ende of this Plantation.[27] John Eliot and Daniel Gookin, who had been appointed by the General Court to be the "superintendent of the Indians of Massachusetts" worked together to fulfill this mission. Their visits to praying towns began with Eliot leading worship. Gookin followed and dealt with disciplinary matters and either made or approved government appointments.

In an effort to teach Native Americans the Christian faith, John Eliot learned the Algonquin language, which he mistakenly called the Massachusett language.[28] He translated the entire Bible into the Algonquin language in 1663, the first Bible printed in America. He also composed a Native primer and psalter and acquired enough fluency to be able to preach in Algonquin. However, Eliot's first effort at mission evangelism Tinker rates as "an embarrassing failure."[29] He says that it was necessary for the General Court of the Bay Colony to come to Eliot's rescue by making blasphemy a capital crime and banning traditional sacred ceremonies such as the powwow.

The first "praying towns" were established in 1646, fifteen years after Eliot began his ministry in Roxbury and roughly ten years after the Treaty of Hartford was signed. New Englanders supported the creation of these towns because they established a buffer between the settlers and the Natives and reduced the likelihood of renewed warfare. Housing Native Americans in these towns was also a way to lessen economic competition. Natives were willing to move into these towns because it was becoming increasingly difficult for them to live in their traditional ways as the white population pushed deeper and deeper into their homeland. John Eliot wanted to establish these towns in order to advance his mission to "civilize and Christianize the Indians."

Tinker suggests that the model for praying towns came from the Spanish missionaries who had established *reduccions* in California and the southwest.[30] *Reduccions* were housing units located within the mission compound. Native peoples housed in these units were removed from their own communities and families and placed under the complete control and oversight of Christian missionaries.

"Praying Indians" and "red Christians," as residents of the praying towns were known, were given incentives to live in them. The towns offered residents food, shelter, and safety, all of which were becoming increasingly scarce. In addition, residents could own land if they renounced tribal language, stopped wearing traditional dress, forswore their own spiritual rituals and customs, learned English, and became Christians.

The first step in welcoming Native American men into the "civilized" societies of the praying towns was to cut their hair short. It is difficult to overstate the importance of this act. It meant putting the mark of "civilization" on the men and shearing them of their native spirituality and identity. The second step was to require "proper" (Western) attire. The third step was to prohibit the use of native languages, including names. These requirements were not superficial. They were calculated steps that fit into the pattern of cultural genocide that was clearly part of Eliot's mission.

Eliot was thorough in his planning and left little to chance. In order to undermine tribal patterns of leadership and authority, he identified tribal members over whom he could exercise control and elevated them to positions of leadership. He also promoted monogamy as Christian virtue, thereby undermining traditional patterns of family life, which were established as a tribal way to care for widows and orphans. The following rules attest to the degree to which all aspects of life in the praying towns was regulated:

1. If any man shall be idle for a week, or at most a fortnight, he shall be fined five shillings.
2. If any unmarried man shall lie with a young woman unmarried, he shall be fined five shillings.
3. If any man shall beat his wife, his hands shall be tied behind him, and he shall be carried to the place of justice and punished severely.
4. Every young man, if not another's servant, and if unmarried, shall be compelled to set up a wigwam and plant himself, and not shift up and down in other wigwams.
5. If any woman shall not have her hair tied up, but hang loose, or be cut as a man's hair, she shall pay five shillings.
6. If any woman shall be with naked breasts, she shall pay two shillings.
7. All men that wear long locks shall pay five shillings.
8. If any man shall crack lice between his teeth, he shall pay five shillings.[31]

Although a stated goal of the praying towns was to "civilize and Christianize the Indians," white settlers never intended to allow "red Christians" to become members of white churches or to move into white communities. Eliot made clear his intention to marginalize the Natives in his book, *The Christian Commonwealth: or, The Civil Policy of the Rising Kingdom of Christ, 1659.*[32] The tone of the book was patronizing toward the "poor, blind, and dark Indians," as well as a vitriolic attack on "that dirty Roman Religion." King Charles II wisely refused to allow the book to be published, and eventually Eliot had to retract it.

By 1675, there were three praying towns in Connecticut with 350 residents, and fourteen praying towns in Massachusetts Bay Colony, home to approximately four thousand residents. Tinker insists that the intent behind the praying towns was to introduce Native Americans to an English-style economy and work ethic, subvert their traditional division of labor, and create economically dependent client communities.[33] The failure of the praying towns to accomplish these goals contributed to the abandonment of the project in 1675.

However, Vine Deloria Jr. reports that in Massachusetts some, but not all, of the praying towns evolved into regular townships. Any shortcomings evidenced in the towns were blamed on failings of Native American character. In time these "failings" provided justification for the State of Massachusetts to place all the Native towns under trusteeship. By 1870, Massachusetts had eliminated self-government for all Native communities in the state and abolished the property rights of individual Native Americans.[34]

Increase Mather and King Philip's War

King Philip's War (1675–1676) was brief and bloody. Indeed, it was by some measures the bloodiest war ever fought on American soil.[35] Plymouth Colony lost eight percent of its men during the war. The Native population of southern New England sustained a loss estimated to be between sixty and eighty percent. At the war's end, Chief Metacom (called King Philip by the English), leader of the Wampanoag Tribe, was decapitated, and his head displayed on a pole in Plymouth for twenty years. Stories of Native American atrocities circulated among the colonists and their descendants for the next century, and it took one hundred years for the economy of New England to recover to a pre-war level.[36]

The spiritual impact of the war was no less profound than its economic impact. It seems likely that the trauma of this war sowed the seeds for the Great Awakening. Increase Mather, a leading Boston minister who at one time served as president of Harvard, wrote a controversial interpretation of King Philip's War that I believe prepared the way for the spiritual revival that was soon to come.

Mather's *Brief History of the Warr with the Indians in New England, 1676* was not well received by his contemporaries.[37] Michael Hall tells us in *The Last American Puritan: The Life of Increase Mather* that William Hubbard wrote an account of the war that went through seven editions, while Mather's book was obsolete even in his own day.[38] What makes Mather's account of the war of enduring interest is that it embodied the mythology of the United States as a nation born out of crisis. He depicted the war as a cosmic struggle between good and evil. He argued that the war was a chastening rod of the Lord, but he also assured his readers that God had not abandoned New England.

The opening sentence of *A Brief History* sets the tone for all that follows:

> That the Heathen People amongst whom we live, and whose land the Lord God of our Fathers hath given to us for rightful Possession, have at sundry times been plotting mischievous devices against that part of the English Israel which is seated in these goings down of the Sun, no man that is an inhabitant of any considerable standing, can be ignorant.[39]

Mather quickly moves from this righteous beginning to label Metacom and his followers "barbarous murders" who "live in a swamp." Then he decries the naked bodies of English men and women lying exposed in open fields. The contrast between the subhuman species living in the swamps and the exposed bodies of slain civilized Christians in open fields gives Mather license to declare that on that "Day of Humiliation, the Lord thereby declared from heaven that he expects something else from his People besides fasting and prayer."[40]

Throughout the book Mather labels indigenous peoples "barbarians" and accuses them of "treachery," while praising his fellow Christians for having established churches among them. Yet he also castigates believers for failing to convert all the "heathens" to Christ. Mather interprets the war as just punishment of the "pagans" and divine judgment on the Christians. He calls Christians to a period of intense introspection and presumably renewed dedication.

King Philip's War virtually cleared southern New England of its aboriginal population. In its aftermath the English established themselves as the dominant people. Eric Schultz and Michael Tougias contend in *King Philip's War: The History and Legacy of America's Forgotten Conflict* that "King Philip's War became the brutal model for how the United States would come to deal with its native population. Later names like Tippecanoe, Black Hawk's War, the Trail of Tears, the Salt Creek Massacre, the Red River War, and Wounded Knee all took place under the long, violent shadow of King Philip's War."[41]

King Philip's War decimated, but did not exterminate, the Wampanoag peoples. Today they are an important part of New England's population. However, the impact of the war was so profound that it would be 253 years after Philip's death—1929—before the Wampanoag would hold their first powwow of the modern era.[42]

The image of Native Americans began to change in white culture with James Fenimore Cooper's *Leatherstocking Tales*, a series of five novels published between 1826 and 1841. Cooper was the first major

U.S. writer to portray Native Americans in his work. Henry Wadsworth Longfellow's poem, *The Song of Hiawatha*, published in 1855, featured a Native American hero. At the end of the poem, Hiawatha welcomes the "Black-Robe chief" and becomes a Christian. The poem was an immediate success and sold over fifty thousand copies. Later, in 1863, Abraham Lincoln established the national holiday of Thanksgiving—a cathartic celebration of nationhood honoring the good relationship between Native Americans and settlers who shared a feast together. It was an image that neither Increase Mather nor his son Cotton Mather could have anticipated or understood.[43]

NOTES

[1]Elizabeth Cook-Lynn, *Anti-Indianism in Modern America: a Voice from Tatekeya's Earth* (Urbana: University of Illinois Press, 2007), 5.

[2]"The First Charter of Virginia; April 10, 1606," 2008 Lillian Goldman Law Library. The Federal and State Constitutions, Colonial Charters, and Other Organic Laws of States. http://www.avalon.law.yale.edu/17th_century/va01.asp. Accessed 6/2/2014·

[3]Stanley Johnson, "John Donne and the Virginia Company," *ELH*, Vol. 14, No. 2, 1947, 128. Published by The John Hopkins University Press. http://www.jstor.org/stable/2871650.

[4]R.S. Thomas, "The Religious Element in the Settlement of Jamestown in 1607," Historical address delivered before the sixth annual council of the Diocese of Southern Virginia, June 10, 1898. Transcribed by Wayne Kempton, Archivist of the Episcopal Diocese of New York, 2007. The Franklin Press Company. http//anglicanhistory.org/usa/misc/thomas_jamestown1898.html. Accessed 5/17/2014.

[5]Ibid., 8.

[6]Ibid., 14.

[7]Alan Taylor, "Virginia, 1570–1650," *in American Colonies* (New York: Viking, 2001), 130.

[8]Helen C. Rountree, "Powhatan Priests and English Rectors: World Views and Congregations in Conflict," *American Indian Quarterly*, Vol. 16, Issue 4, 1992, 485–500. Lincoln: University of Nebraska Press. http://www.jstor.org/stable/1185294?seq=1#page_scan_tab_contents.

[9]Peter Linebaugh and Marcus Rediker, *The Many-Headed Hydra: Sailors, Slaves, Commoners, and the Hidden History of the Revolutionary Atlantic,* reprint ed. (Boston: Beacon Press, 2013), 33.

[10]Ibid., italics original, 33. See also "The Second Charter of Virginia, May 23, 1609," The Avalon Project: Documents in Law, History and Diplomacy, Yale Law School, Lillian Goldman Law Library. http://wwwavalon.law.yale.edu/17th_century/va02asp. Accessed 6/25/2014.

[11]Kirkpatrick Sale, *The Conquest of Paradise: Christopher Columbus and the Columbian Legacy* (New York: Alfred A. Knopf, 1990), 277.

[12]Linebaugh and Rediker, *Many-Headed Hydra,* 34–35.

[13]Robert A. Williams, Jr., *Savage Anxieties: The Invention of Western Civilization* (New York: Palgrave Macmillan, 2012), 194. Williams cites Alexander Whitaker, *Good News from Virginia,* 24–27; quoted in Robert F. Berkhofer, Jr., *The White Man's Indian: Images of the American Indian from Columbus to the Present* 5 (1979). See fn 35 on 246.

[14]John Donne, "A Sermon Preached to the Honorable Company of the Virginia Plantation. 13 November 1622. Citation: "The Sermons of John Donne," vol.4, no. 10. Public domain. Electronically reproduction: University of California Press, 1959.

Published digital: Brigham Young University, 2004–05. http://cdm15999.contentdm.oclc. org/cdm/ref/collection/JohnDonne/id/3178.

See also Williams, "The Language of Savagery at Jamestown," *Savage Anxieties*, which also discusses Waterhouse, 192–96.

[15]Edward Waterhouse, "A Declaration of the State of Affairs of the Colony and~A Relation of the Barbarous Massacre," *The Records of the Virginia Company*, 553. Part of the Thomas Jefferson Papers at the Library of Congress: Series 8, Virginia Records Manuscripts. 1606 to 1737. http://www.loc.gov/resource/mtj8.vc03/?sp=573. Accessed 11/8/2015.

[16]Ibid., 557.

[17]J. Frederick Fausz, *The "Barbarous Massacre" Reconsidered: The Powhatan Uprising of 1622 and the Historians* (Baltimore: Maryland Historical Society, 1978).

[18]Ibid., 576.

[19]Taylor, *American Colonies*, uses this phrase to describe the New England colonies, 178.

[20]H. Richard Niebuhr, *The Kingdom of God in America* (New York: Harper & Row, Publishers, 1937, Harper Torchbook edition, 1959), 56.

[21]William Bradford, *Of Plymouth Plantation*, An Electronic Edition, William Bradford 1590–1657, 30. Original Source: *Bradford's History of Plymouth Plantation, 1606–1646.*, ed. William T. Davis (New York: Charles Scribner's Sons, 1908). http://mith.umd.edu/eada/html/display.php?docs=bradford_history.xml. Accessed 12/13/2015.

[22]George E. Tinker, *Missionary Conquest: The Gospel and Native American Cultural Genocide* (Minneapolis: Fortress Press, 1993), 15.

[23]Ibid., 23. Tinker cites Edward Winslow, "Good News from England" (1624), in *Chronicles of the Pilgrim Fathers of the Colony of Plymouth from 1602 to 1625*, ed. Alexander Young (Boston, 1841), 336–43. See fn 16 on 133.

[24]Linebaugh and Rediker, *Many-Headed Hydra*, 91.

[25]"An Epitome or Brief History of the Pequot War," John Mason and Paul Royster, eds., Open access at DigitalCommons@University of Nebraska-Lincoln. http://digitalcommons.unl.edu/cgi/viewcontent.cgi?article=1042&context=etas. Accessed 11/10/2015.

[26]Nathaniel Philbrick, *Mayflower: A Story of Courage, Community and War* (New York: Viking Press, 2006), 179.

[27]"Charter of Massachusetts Bay 1629," in *American History from the Revolution to Reconstruction and beyond*. University of Groningen. http://www.let.rug.nl/usa/documents/1600-1650/charter-of-massachusetts-bay-1629.php. Accessed 12/13/2015.

[28]Algonquin refers both to a language and to a large group of tribes that speak a related dialect. John Eliot's confusion, while understandable, is indicative of a larger problem. Human beings think and live through language. However genuine Eliot's desire was to translate the Bible into Algonquin, his translation was not only an attempt to convey a new faith to Native Americans; it was also an attempt to undermine their cultures.

[29]Tinker, "John Eliot: Conversion, Colonialism, and the Oppression of Language," in *Missionary Conquest*, 29.

[30]Ibid., 18–20.

[31]Nipmuc Indian Association of Connecticut, "The Praying Towns," Historical Series 2, Second Edition, 1995. http://www.nativetech.org/Nipmuc/praytown.html. Accessed June 4, 2014

[32]John Eliot, *The Christian Commonwealth: or, The Civil Policy of the Rising Kingdom of Christ, 1659*. Paul Royster (editor and depositor), An Online Electronic Text Edition, Lincoln,: University of Nebraska Press. http//www.digitalcommons.uni.edu/

libraryscience/19. It is believed that Eliot wrote this before the execution of King Charles I on January 30, 1649, but the book was not published until 1659. In May, 1660, after the accession of Charles II to the throne, Eliot issued an apology for his attack upon Catholics. In the Preface to the book Eliot conveys a millennial expectation of Christ's coming and the establishment of a Christian (read Protestant) government that will bring peace and unity on earth, after "beating in pieces that dirty Roman Religion and all civil States, which are complicated with it," iv. In the Preface, Eliot also states with humility that the Lord has called him "to instruct our poor, blind, and dark Indians, in the good knowledge of the Lord," ix. In the same passage he vows "to endeavor with all his might to bring them under the government of the Lord."

[33]Tinker, *Missionary Conquest*, 32–33.

[34]Vine Deloria, Jr., "Property and Self-Government as Educational Initiatives," in Vine Deloria, Jr. and Daniel R. Wildcat, *Power and Place: Indian Education in America* (Golden, CO: Fulcrum Resources, 2001), 103–4.

[35]Philbrick, *Mayflower*, 332. According to Philbrick the United States lost just under one percent of its adult male population during the forty-five months of World War II. The casualty rate during the Civil War was between four and five percent.

[36]Eric B. Schultz and Michael J. Tougias, *King Philip's War: The History and Legacy of America's Forgotten Conflict* (Woodstock, VT: The Countryman Press, 1999).

[37]Increase Mather, *A Brief History of the Warr with the Indians in New England, 1676*. Paul Royseter (editor and depositor) DigitalCommons@University of Nebraska, Lincoln, an Online Electronic Edition. http://digitalcommons.unl.edu/libraryscience/31/. Accessed 7/8/2014.

[38]Michael G. Hall, *The Last American Puritan: The Life of Increase Mather* (Middletown, CT: Wesleyan University Press, 1998), 126.

[39]Mather, *Brief History*, 9.

[40]Ibid., 12.

[41]Schultz and Tougias, *King Philip's War*, 1.

[42]Ibid., 2.

[43]The first Thanksgiving was likely a feast provided by Native Americans and shared with New Englanders who were on the brink of starvation. The narrative that the New Englanders provided the feast and invited the Natives is most likely a myth.

5

Christian Collusion with Colonial Conquest

To tell the story of the mainline church's collusion with the government to make war on Native Americans, I have arranged this chapter around a series of twelve episodes and vignettes: (1) the Great Awakening and Missionary Zeal, (2) the Cornwall Mission School, (3) the Civilization Fund, (4) Andrew Jackson's Indian–removal policy, (5) the Marshall Trilogy, (6) Westward expansion and Indian wars, (7) Indian boarding schools, (8) Henry Pratt and other Friends of the Indians, (9) Native American resistance, (10) federal policies, (11) the present, and (12) pointing the way.

The Great Awakening and Missionary Zeal

As the nation expanded, new divisions in the white population became evident. The "Old Lights," the established and entrenched leadership in New England, could not prevent the "New Lights," which were associated with religious revivals on the frontiers of colonial society, from shining. Immigration, religious schisms, denominational conflicts, antagonisms between Puritan New England and the Middle Colonies, and social divisions between the rich and the poor contributed to reshaping the religious landscape of eighteenth-century America and coalesced in the Great Awakening, a religious revival that began in 1735 on the frontier of Massachusetts and Connecticut.

During this period, as John Wesley famously said, Christian hearts "were strangely warmed." In the decade between 1735 and 1745, fiery orators like Jonathan Edwards, George Whitfield, and Charles Finney awakened the nation to a new awareness of God's presence. Sanctification, the inward experience of God's saving grace, assumed a central place in the lives of the faithful. Sanctified believers thought that they were commissioned to contribute to the realization of God's reign in history by bringing the light of salvation to the ignorant natives. For them, the saving truth of the gospel was not merely a truth; it was The Truth.

The commission attributed to Jesus, "Go therefore and make disciples of all nations," (Mt. 28:19) became the template for a global mission movement.[1] The "angel of Macedonia" who had once summoned Paul (Acts 16:9) and who had called the English to Jamestown was once again calling the church to new mission fields. Responding to the vision of a redeemed (Christian) humanity, global mission agencies sprang up in Europe and the United States: the Society for the Propagation of the Gospel in Foreign Parts was founded in 1701; the London Missionary Society (1795); the Church Missionary Society (1799); the American Board of Commissioners for Foreign Missions (1812); and the Wesleyan Methodist Society (1813).

Religion scholar R.S. Sugirtharajah contends: "The rise of Protestant countries as colonial powers, the vigorous mushrooming of Protestant mission-sending agencies, and the recuperation of missionary texts, were all inextricably mixed."[2] There was, he suggests, a "collusion between colonialism and exegesis" that, in an age of imperial expansion, allowed "a Western ethnocentrism...[to be] pass[ed]...off as universalism."[3] Missiologist David J. Bosch writes of this era: "Europe and North America were the solid beacons of orientation, the models for the non-Christian world still to be brought into the orbit of Christianity."[4]

Churches in Europe and in the United States adopted a strategy of "mission in six continents." This plan called for sending Christian missionaries to all corners of the world, and bringing people of color from all parts of the world to schools in the United States and Europe to learn the ways of Western civilization and Christianity. One of these schools was the famous Cornwall Mission School in Cornwall, Connecticut, which John Ridge and Elias Boudinot, both members of important families in the Cherokee Nation, attended. Later Ridge and Boudinot would play critical roles in the forced migration of the Cherokee Tribe under Andrew Jackson's Indian Removal Act. Their experience at the Cornwall Mission School gives us insight into the interplay of religion, race, and gender in early nineteenth-century Protestant America.

The Cornwall Mission School

The American Board of Commissioners for Foreign Missions established the Cornwall Mission School in 1817. In the minutes of the board, Secretary Rufus Anderson explained that the mission of the school was: "The education, in our country, of heathen youths, in such manner as, with subsequent professional instruction, will qualify them to be useful missionaries, physicians, surgeons, schoolmasters, or interpreters; and to communicate to the heathen nations such knowledge in agriculture and the arts as may prove the means of promoting Christianity and civilization."[5] The curriculum was thoroughly Western and included study of the classics, mathematics, reading and writing, learning trades and theology. Before the school closed its doors in 1826, it educated approximately one hundred students who spoke twenty-four different native languages.

While attending Cornwall, Ridge and Boudinot each met and married white women. Such interracial marriages were clear violations of social norms and religious sanctions, though not a violation of the law. Curiously, the law forbade white men from marrying Native American women, but it said nothing about white women marrying Native men.

When John Ridge and Sarah Northrup exchanged their sacred vows, the editors of the Litchfield newspaper, *American Eagle,* declared that "affliction, mortification and disgrace are the relatives of the young woman ... who made herself a *squaw."* The newspaper called the marriage an "unnatural connection" and asked if the school was trying to engineer "a new kind of *missionary machinery."*[6] To defend the school, its administrators had to publically condemn the marriage and promise that such a scandalous arrangement would never happen again.

However, soon after John Ridge and Sarah Northrup were married, Harriett Gold told her father, Dr. Gold, a prominent member of the community and an important contributor to the school, that she and Elias Boudinot planned to get married. He forbade it. But when she, his only daughter, professed that she would lose the will to live if he would not allow it, he relented—provided that it would be kept secret. When word got out, the school denounced the couple's plan and accused those who condoned it of criminal intent, adding that they were insulting the Christian community and sporting with the sacred institution of marriage. Public protest swelled, church bells rang, and Harriett's effigy was laid on a funeral pyre in the public square and set ablaze by her own brother. She refused to back down.

On Sunday morning, Harriet Gold took her accustomed place in the choir. The pastor demanded that she leave. She walked out with her head held high into the waiting arms of Elias. The two were married in the Gold home on March 28, 1826. The school shut its doors later that same year. In the board minutes Secretary Anderson explained that the lack of funds and the decline in enrollment of Native American students were contributing causes. He did not mention either marriage.

The Civilization Fund

In the 1790s, one of the most pressing "problems" facing the new national government was deciding the future status of Native Americans. At issue was the fact that Natives possessed the land, and whites wanted the land. However, it was not simply a matter of unvarnished greed that motivated the whites. The fate of the republic depended on acquiring the land. According to the prevailing political theory of John Locke, only a society based on private property could guarantee public morality, political independence, and social stability. But the settlers could not simply take Native American land, as kings had once taken their land. They needed a justifying rationale, and found it in the philosophy of John Locke.

Locke theorized that civilization was the perfection of the state of nature. While all people living in the state of nature were equal, people who remained in the state of nature were uncivilized barbarians and the enemies of civilization. Since Native Americans did not own private property or have a form of government recognized by Christians, they were uncivilized by definition.

Seizing upon Locke's bifurcation of who was civilized and who was uncivilized, Thomas Jefferson proposed that it would be mutually beneficial to both parties if the Natives exchanged their land for the benefit of receiving white civilization and Christianity. Jefferson called this exchange a "coincidence of interests." By contrast, in *Education for Extinction*, David Wallace Adams, an associate professor of education at Cleveland State University, calls the exchange a "convenient conjoinment of greed and philanthropy."[7]

Jefferson's plan to exchange Christian civilization for Native American land evolved, and in 1818 the House Committee on Indian Affairs urged Congress to create a "Civilization Fund." The purpose of the fund was to:

> Put into the hands of their Indian children the primer and the hoe, and they will naturally, in time, take hold of the plow; and, as their minds become enlightened and expand, the Bible will be their book, and they will grow up in the habits of morality and industry, leave the chase to those whose minds are less cultivated, and become useful members of society.[8]

Congress allocated $10,000 to the Civilization Fund for schools on reservations to be run by Christian denominations. However, some Christian denominations refused to participate because they believed that the plan violated the principle of the separation of church and state. Whites who simply wanted to get rid of the Native Americans and take their land also strongly opposed the plan.

Opposition to the Civilization Fund prompted John C. Calhoun, President James Madison's Secretary of State, to devise the first plan for Native removal in 1824. Calhoun proposed that Native Americans would voluntarily exchange their land east of the Mississippi River for land west of it. The plan could be defended on the humanitarian grounds that it saved the Native Americans from extinction, and justified politically as a way to gain control of Native land without bloodshed. However the plan failed to win approval in the House of Representatives.

Andrew Jackson's Indian Removal Policy

The plan for Indian removal received new life when Andrew Jackson took the presidential oath of office on March 4, 1829. The authorizing legislation for Jackson's removal policy was "The Bill for an Exchange of Lands with Indians Residing in Any of the States or Territories and Their Removal West of the Mississippi," which won Senate approval by a vote of 28 to 19. The vote in the House of Representatives was closer, 102 for and 98 against. Jackson signed the bill into law on June 30, 1830. On September 27, 1830, Jackson signed the Treaty of Dancing Rabbit Creek with the Choctaw Nation. It was the first removal treaty under the new law. The Choctaw Nation ceded about 11 million acres of land (now part of Mississippi) in exchange for 15 million acres of land west of the Mississippi (now part of Oklahoma). Tens of thousands of Choctaw walked westward on the Choctaw Trail of Tears. Many died on the journey, made in the dead of winter. The heartless policy of removal continued until 1838, the year of the Cherokee Trail of Tears.

Jackson's successor, Martin Van Buren, continued the removal policy. In 1838, he told Congress: "It affords me sincere pleasure to apprise the Congress of the entire removal of the Cherokee Nation of Indians to their new homes west of the Mississippi. The measures authorized by Congress at its last session have had the happiest effects."[9] During the Jackson and Van Buren administrations, roughly seventy thousand Native Americans lost their homelands and were forced to move to land west of the Mississippi River. By the end of Van Buren's presidency, most of the land east of the Mississippi River was owned by white people.

The Marshall Trilogy[10]

Congress authorized the forced marches that moved Native Americans from their homelands east of the Mississippi River to territories to the west of it. But it was the U.S. Supreme Court under the leadership of Chief Justice John Marshall that created the legal fiction that made the appropriation of Native American lands lawful. In three landmark decisions, the Marshall court established the legal framework that remains the basis of federal Indian policy. The three cases, known as the Marshall Trilogy, are *Johnson v. McIntosh* (1823), *Cherokee Nation v. Georgia* (1831), and *Worcester v. Georgia* (1832). Robert Williams identifies the two organizing principles in these three cases as "white superiority and Indian savagery."[11] The central tenet in the justices' arguments is that with discovery comes authority, and with authority, the right of conquest.[12] Williams says that as legal precedent, Marshall's opinion in these three cases was treated with "oracular status."[13] When the church apologized to Native Americans, it repudiated its mission to "civilize and Christianize" them and when it renounced the Doctrine of Discovery, it challenged the veracity of the Marshall Trilogy.

Robert Williams writes in *Like a Loaded Weapon* that "as measured by today's racial sensibilities, *Johnson v. McIntosh* has to be considered one of the most thoroughly racist, nonegalitarian, undemocratic, and stereotype-infused decisions ever issued by the Supreme Court."[14] Williams contends that this decision provided legal sanction to the notion of white racial superiority and white dictatorship over an entire continent that white Europeans imagined they discovered and over the "nonconsenting and non-European peoples" who lived there.[15] Furthermore, it violated contemporary understandings and international agreements recognizing human rights, and it did so in the name of an antiquated Doctrine of Discovery.

Johnson v. McIntosh[16] involved a land dispute between two white men—no Native Americans were represented. Johnson inherited land from his father, who bought it from the Piankehaw Indians. McIntosh was later granted title to the same property in a sale by the U.S. government. The high court had to decide: Did Native Americans possess title to their land? If they did, then Johnson's claim was valid. Chief Justice John Marshall reasoned that it was not. The Doctrine of Discovery, Marshall said, entitled the "great nations of Europe" with their "superior" character, religion, and genius, to claim the land. Guided by this reasoning, the Court recognized McIntosh's claim and invalidated Johnson's.

To give added support to his decision, Chief Justice Marshall wrote in the *Johnson* decision that Native Americans had "limited sovereignty." He meant by this that they lived upon the land, but they did not hold title to it. Therefore, the government was justified in taking the land on the grounds that the superior culture and religion of the settlers was reasonable compensation to the Native Americans. In a commentary on this ruling, Deloria wrote that Marshall's justification "is wholly a fiction deriving from earlier claims by Spain and Portugal that the pope, as Christ's representative on earth, had given them claim to the lands of the Western Hemisphere."[17] Fiction though it was, the decision established precedent and stands as one of the most important Native American law cases in the history of the United States.

Cherokee Nation v. Georgia (1831) was precipitated by white prospectors who discovered gold on Cherokee land in 1829.[18] The state of Georgia supported the prospectors when they filed their claims. The Cherokee Nation turned to the courts for protection, arguing that the claims were a violation of a treaty agreement between the United States and the Cherokee Nation. Therefore, they believed, the Supreme Court had original jurisdiction in the resolution of this dispute. However, Chief Justice Marshall found that the Cherokee Nation was not an independent nation, but rather a "domestic dependent nation," and asserted that the Cherokees' relationship to the government was, "that of a ward to his guardian. Indians look to the government for protection; rely on its kindness and power; appeal to it for relief of their wants; and address the President as their Great Father." Marshall reasoned that the Cherokee Nation had no standing before the Supreme Court and no basis on which to file a claim. The decision effectively vacated all federal treaties with all Native tribes and nations.

In a concurring opinion, Associate Justice William Johnson wrote:

> When the eastern coast of this continent, and especially the part we inhabit, was discovered, finding it occupied by a race of hunters, connected in a society but scarcely a semblance of organic government; the right was extended to the absolute appropriation of the territory, the annexation of it to the domain of the discoverer. It cannot be questioned that the right of sovereignty, as well as the soil, was notoriously asserted and exercised by the European discoverers. From that source we derive our rights, and there is not an instance of cessation of land from an Indian nation, in which the right of sovereignty is mentioned as part of the matter ceded.[19]

After the court handed down its verdict in the Cherokee Nation case, the Georgia legislature enacted a law that required all white people living on Cherokee land to be licensed by the state. Samuel Worcester, a missionary commissioned by the American Board of Commissioners for Foreign Missions who lived with the Cherokee Nation, was one of the missionaries targeted by this legislation. Since neither Worcester nor any of the other Christian missionaries was licensed, they were subject to arrest.

Worcester wore many hats. As a missionary his duty was "to make the whole tribe English in their language, civilized in their habits, and Christian in their religion."[20] Worcester also served as the local administrator of the Civilization Fund and as the U.S. Postmaster, which made him a federal employee and exempted him from prosecution by the State of Georgia. But the governor of Georgia disregarded the exemption and had Worcester and Samuel Butler, another Christian missionary, arrested. When the case went to trial, the American Board of Commissioners for Foreign Missions celebrated Samuel Worcester as a martyr but did not pay his legal fees. The Cherokee Tribe, however, did help meet these expenses, and a tribal attorney represented him in court.

In this the third case in the Marshall Trilogy, Chief Justice Marshall declared that the Georgia law under which Worcester had been convicted was "repugnant, null and void." The Governor of Georgia refused to release Worcester. President Jackson sided with the governor, and dismissively said, "Marshall made his ruling, now let him enforce it."

Worcester v. Georgia has enduring legal interest because it was the first time that the Supreme Court had to address the important issue of states' rights. John Marshall's ruling established the supremacy of the federal law and limited the rights of states. The ruling also limited Native American claims to sovereignty and property and expanded the power of the federal government in Native affairs.

Robert Williams identifies four principal elements of the "Marshall Model of Indian Rights" that were established by the Marshall Trilogy.[21] First, the Marshall model is based on the notion of white superiority and Native American racial inferiority. Second, by reference to the Doctrine of Discovery the model defines white racial supremacy over the United States. Third, the model relies on judicially validated claims of Native American inferiority to justify the assertion of white privilege. Finally, relying on the Doctrine of Discovery makes it impossible for the justices to do anything to protect Native rights because the Doctrine of Discovery predates the Constitution. When issuing apologies to Native Americans, mainline denominations repudiated the Doctrine of Discovery, and they implicitly recognized the right of indigenous peoples to own land and to have the right to self-governance, positioning themselves to challenge the Marshall model.

Westward Expansion and Indian Wars

The so-called "Indian Wars" are documented in many places. A summary is sufficient to give a context for this section. The fight against the Seminole Tribe in Florida lasted eight years and ended in 1840. The Navajo conflicts began in 1849 and went on until 1863. The Sioux Wars in the Great Plains extended from 1854 to 1890. The Apache campaigns, which stretched from Texas to California, commenced in 1851 and dragged on into the first decade of the twentieth century. As noted in a previous chapter, there is no evidence that Christian missionaries engaged directly in the systematic killing of Native Americans during this period except for Colonel John Chivington.[22] Christians were deeply involved in these wars and bear some responsibility for them. However, the main focus of the church's anti-Native campaign was in the educational arena.

Indian Boarding Schools

In 1869, prompted in part by the church's concern for Native Americans, President Ulysses S. Grant proposed a "Peace Plan." He entrusted the administration of the plan to what he thought were high-minded and well-intentioned Protestant denominations intent on assimilating Native Americans into white society and Christian culture. Francis Paul Prucha says that when the Board of Indian Commissioners was appointed, "there was no Catholic on the Board, and there was no indication that one was seriously considered—despite the long interest of the Catholic Church in Indian affairs."[23]

Not incidentally, the timing of Grant's Peace Plan coincided with the completion of the transcontinental railroad and the rapid westward expansion of the nation. In his annual address to Congress in 1869, President Grant reflected on what the future held for "civilized settlements" that would come into contact with Native American tribes. Grant told members of Congress: "No matter what ought to be the relations between such settlements and the aboriginals, the fact is they do not harmonize well, and one or the other has to give way in the end. A system that looks to the extinction of a race is too horrible for a nation to adopt without entailing upon itself the wrath of all Christendom and engendering in the citizens a disregard for human life and the rights of others, dangerous to society."[24] As the president saw it, the Native Americans could be neither slaughtered nor allowed to live with whites who would soon be invading their territory. The peace plan was a third way.

The purpose of the Board of Indian Commissioners was to oversee the operation of the Indian boarding schools and to make recommendations to Congress. Commissioners came from twelve Christian denominations that "saw no impropriety in educating the 'savages,' and Christianizing the 'heathen,' and rescuing the 'godless' by educating Indians in the ways of Anglo-American religion, culture, technology, and lifeways."[25] In the words of David Adams, with the start of the Indian boarding schools,

> The war against the Indians had now entered a new phase. Conquering a continent and its aboriginal peoples had been a bloody business, and for Christian people, not without moral discomfort. Now the war against the savages would be waged in a gentler fashion. The next Indian war would be ideological and psychological, and it would be waged against the children.[26]

The Commissioners questioned neither the need to assimilate the Native Americans into white Christian culture nor their ability to complete this mission. In their Twelfth Annual Report, the Board of Indian Commissioners assessed the situation:

> The most reliable statistics prove conclusively that the Indian population taken as a whole, instead of dying out under the light and contact with civilization, as has been generally supposed, is steadily increasing. The Indian is evidently

destined to live as long as the white race, or until he becomes absorbed and assimilated with his pale brethren…

As we must have him among us, self-interest, humanity, and Christianity require that we should accept the situation, and go resolutely at work to make him a safe and useful factor in our body politic.

As a savage we cannot tolerate him any more than as a half-civilized parasite, wanderer, or vagabond. The only alternative left is to fit him by education for civilized life.[27]

The Commissioners and their many allies did not question the need to mold Native Americans for Christian civilization by teaching them English, respect for Euro-American law, and U.S. patriotism. Commissioner Thomas Morgan nicely summarized the philosophy of the day when, in an address to the Lake Mohonk Conference in, 1892 he said: "We must either fight the Indians, or feed them, or educate them. To fight them is cruel; to feed them is wasteful; to educate them is humane, economic, and Christian."[28]

The Peace Plan was not without controversy. Commissioners were not well supported, either by the administration or by members of Congress. Nonetheless, the plan was defended as a cost-effective way to deal with the "Indian problem." Carl Schurz, the United States Secretary of the Interior from 1877 to 1881, calculated that it would cost nearly $1,000,000 to kill a Native in warfare, but only $1,200 to educate a Native child for eight years in school. Henry Tiller, who followed Schurz as Secretary of the Interior, estimated that over a ten-year period, the annual cost of continuing war with the Native Americans and protecting the frontier communities would be around $22 million, nearly four times the cost of educating thirty thousand Native children annually.

To expedite the entrance of Native Americans into civilization, the Board of Indian Commissioners advocated granting Native Americans full citizenship. In addition, the board exposed corruption both in the government and on reservations, and they helped initiate a government study of Native American social and economic conditions. This recommendation was not acted on until fifty years later, when John Collier, a member of the Seneca Nation, was appointed Commissioner for the Bureau of Indian Affairs. Finally, in 1928, this study was undertaken by the Institute of Government Research (now The Brookings Institution). This federal report, known as the Merriam Report, was entitled "The Problem of Indian Administration." It became the basis for the Indian New Deal, a policy developed during the Franklin D. Roosevelt administration.

In 1886 there were fifty Indian boarding schools supported by a partnership between the federal government and the participating denominations. The Roman Catholic Church was in charge of thirty-eight of these schools, with a combined enrollment of 2,068 students. The twelve Protestant-run schools had a combined enrollment of five hundred students.[29] The participating denominations were Baptist, Christian, Congregational, Dutch Reformed, Episcopal, Hicksite Friends, Lutheran, Methodist, Presbyterian, and Unitarian. Over the years, the federal money allocated for schooling Native American children steadily increased: $20,000 in 1877, $992,800 in 1885, and $2,936,080 in 1900. School enrollment also climbed: 3,598 students in 1877, 8,143 in 1885, and 21,568 in 1900.

The growth in funding and in enrollment is explained in part by the creation of private off-reservation Indian boarding schools, the first of which was started by Richard Henry Pratt in 1879 in Carlisle, Pennsylvania.

Henry Pratt and Other "Friends of the Indians"

A chief advantage of reservation boarding schools was that they established institutional control over the lives of Native American children. However, the schools were in session only eight or nine months of the year. During summer vacation, on holidays, and at other times during the year the children were allowed to return home. Some agents and policymakers thought that federal money was not being spent well, because the gains made during the school year were being undone when the children were not in school. Efforts to "civilize" and "Christianize" the children were being further compromised when parents or tribal members visited the school. Some agents began advocating for off-reservation schools as a way to reduce family and tribal influences.

The so-called Red River War of 1874 and its aftermath provided the opportunity for those who wanted to establish off-reservation schools to realize their hopes.[30] More a series of skirmishes than a war, the conflict was precipitated by the refusal of some Southern Plains tribes to accept the terms of a treaty confining them to reservations. At the end of the conflict a group of seventy-two Native American prisoners, including Cheyenne, Arapaho, Kiowa, Comanche, and Caddo, were taken to Fort Sill, Oklahoma. Lieutenant Henry Pratt, an officer at Fort Sill, was put in charge of the captives. Pratt put his prisoners in irons and took them by train to Fort Leavenworth, Kansas. While there, he received orders to take his prisoners to Fort Marion in St. Augustine, Florida.

In Florida, Henry Pratt learned about the Hampton Normal and Agricultural Institute School in Hampton, Virginia. This school had been started in 1863 by the Reverend Lewis C. Lockwood, an agent of the American Missionary Association, and two free black teachers. At the end of the Civil War it became one of the Freedom Schools run by the U.S. Freedmen's Bureau for the benefit of former black slaves and poor whites.

Henry Pratt was inspired by the Hampton school and used his contacts in the federal government to secure permission to start a school for Native Americans at an abandoned Army base in Carlisle, Pennsylvania, noting, "To civilize the Indian, get him into civilization. To keep him civilized, let him stay."[31] He approached his work with missionary zeal. In a speech that he gave to a Baptist convention in 1883, Pratt announced: "In Indian civilization, I am a Baptist, because I believe in immersing the Indians in our civilization and when we get them under holding them until they are thoroughly soaked."[32] He told the Nineteenth Annual Conference of Corrections and Charities: "All the Indian there is in the race should be dead. Kill the Indian in him, and save the man." Later in the same speech he explained: "Carlisle has always planted treason to the tribe and loyalty to the nation at large. It has preached against colonizing the Indians, and in favor of individualizing them."[33]

Pratt had a fierce desire to utterly destroy Native American family systems and Native cultures. In this, he staunchly opposed the philosophy that informed both the Freedom Schools and the Indian boarding schools run by the church. George Tinker suggests that Pratt's unrelenting drive to assimilate Natives into white culture was informed at least in part by the end of the so-called Indian Wars.[34] Since the actual physical extermination of Native Americans was no longer possible, another way had to be found to solve the "Indian problem." Assimilation was the answer that Pratt proposed: "Kill the Indian, save the man."

The regimen at Carlisle and at other similar schools seems to have been modeled after the praying towns of colonial New England. When boys arrived at Carlisle, their hair was cut short to mark their entrance into the "civilizing" world of Christian culture. They were dressed in "civilized" western clothing, learned the ways of white culture, celebrated patriotic national holidays, and were taught the basics of reading, writing, and arithmetic. Boys learned trades; girls were schooled in domestic chores. Through the practice of "outing"— sending boys to work on farms or in factories and girls to work in homes as domestic servants—Pratt hoped to hasten Native American assimilation into white culture. Critics of the practice of outing charged that Pratt was simply exploiting child labor.

Henry Pratt's desire to individualize Native Americans and force them to accept the civilized ways of white people was shared by other supposedly well-intentioned whites who called themselves "Friends of the Indians." Ethnologist Alice Fletcher, a leading member of this group, was one of the architects of a key piece of legislation designed with this end in mind—the infamous General Allotment Act of 1887, also known as the Dawes Act, named after its sponsor, Senator Henry Dawes of Massachusetts.

Sponsors of the Dawes Act argued that Native peoples would be assimilated into white culture more quickly if tribal land were broken up and allotted formulaically to families and individuals who would learn to become farmers. Land that was not included in the allotment was designated "surplus land" that white settlers, speculators, and corporations could purchase from the government for a modest fee. Money raised from the sale of the land was placed into a fund administered by the Bureau of Indian Affairs for the benefit of Natives. The fact that much of the land allocated to the Native Americans was of such poor quality that it could not be farmed was beside the point.

When the Dawes Act became law, Fletcher proclaimed: "The Indian may now become a free man; free from the thralldom of the tribe; free from the domination of the reservation system; free to enter into the body of our citizens. This bill may therefore be considered the Magna Carta of the Indians in our country."[35] Senator Dawes declared:

> If you clothe him in his right mind, put him on his own land, furnish him with a little habitation, with a plow, and a rake, and show him how to go to work and use them. Now can you put a guardian around him? You might just as well put a plant in a cellar in the dark and bid it to develop and bear fruit. The only way is to lead him out into the sunshine, and tell him what the sunshine is for, and what the rain comes for, and when to put his seed in the ground.[36]

Before the Dawes Act became law, Native Americans owned 138 million acres. By the time law was repealed in 1934, they owned only 48 million acres. Collectively, they lost 90 million acres of land, and 90,000 Natives became both landless and homeless. Thus, the Dawes Act accomplished its purpose of opening up protected Native American land to white speculators and settlers and undermining Native culture, but it was not the Magna Carta of Native freedom.

Native American Resistance

The authors of the "Harvard Project on American Indian Economic Development" conclude that "by the end of the nineteenth century, the United States effectively exercised an invader's control over Indian nations, lands, resources, and affairs within its boundaries."[37] Paradoxically, however, the Indian boarding school project and other attempts to undermine tribal structures and cultural patterns provoked a pan-tribal movement among Native Americans and strengthened their resolve to achieve self-governance.[38]

The Native Americans' drive for self-governance received support from the highest levels of government when Franklin D. Roosevelt appointed John Collier to be the Commissioner for the Bureau of Indian

Affairs. Collier, a member of the Seneca Tribe, was the architect of the "Indian New Deal," which became law in 1934. Under the auspices of the Indian New Deal, Collier ended funding for off-reservation schools, increased funding for reservation day schools, disbanded the Board of Indian Commissioners, prohibited the sale of Native lands, and re-established tribal authority.[39] In his Annual Report in 1938, Collier wrote:

> For nearly 300 years white American, in our zeal to carve out a nation made to order, have dealt with Indians on the erroneous, yet tragic, assumption that the Indians are a dying race—to be liquidated. We took away their best lands; broke treaty promises; tossed them the most nearly worthless scraps of a continent that had once been wholly theirs. But we did not liquidate them.

Collier also noted that in the past eight years the Native American population had increased at almost twice the rate of the American population as a whole. He declared an end to talk of the "Indian problem," and affirmed Native tribes as semi-autonomous entities. Then he said:

> We, therefore, define our Indian policy somewhat as follows: So productively to use moneys appropriated by Congress for Indians as to enable them, on good, adequate lands of their own, to earn decent livelihoods and lead self-respecting lives, organized in harmony with their own aims and ideals, as an integral part of American life.[40]

The Indian New Deal did not have unqualified support either in Congress or among Native Americans, it was not an unqualified success, but it did have real benefits for Natives. It allowed for religious freedom, contributed to the revival of traditional practices, helped tribes consolidate their property and acquire new land, and promoted Native self-governance.

Then in the 1950s, the Bureau of Indian Affairs introduced its Urban Indian Relocation Program, which was designed to entice Native Americans to leave reservations and move to urban areas. As a result, many Natives traded reservation poverty for urban poverty. The U.S. government also ran a companion program called *termination* from 1954 until 1970.[41] This program gave the government the authority to determine which tribes were ready for assimilation into the general population. The termination policy applied both to tribes and to individuals. Once the determination was made that a tribe or person was no longer an "Indian," they were stripped of their identity and all treaty relationships. They no longer qualified for treaty-obligated financial payments. Treaty land protections evaporated under the termination policy. A new solution had been found to the old "Indian problem": the U.S. government could simply cull the rolls until there were no more Native Americans.

The Civil Rights Movement of the 1960s and 1970s found fertile ground among Native Americans, where it inspired a new era of political activism. Of the many Native American organizations that have come into existence since the 1960s, the best known is the American Indian Movement (AIM). In 1972, AIM members seized the Bureau of Indian Affairs in Washington, D.C. The next year, AIM members and a number of other Natives were involved in a standoff with agents from the Federal Bureau of Investigation at Wounded Knee, South Dakota, where in 1890 the U.S. Army's Seventh Calvary had slaughtered Lakotas.

Today the Wounded Knee Memorial Ride is an annual pilgrimage that commemorates the 1890 journey of Chief Big Foot and his people. The case of Leonard Peltier, a member of the Anishinabe-Dakota, reflects the present conflict between Native Americans and the government. The 1973 standoff lasted twenty-one days and both Native Americans and federal agents were killed. Peltier was charged with killing two federal agents and is now serving two consecutive life sentences for causing their deaths. In 2001, in response to appeals and pressure from Native Americans and civil rights activists, President Bill Clinton considered granting Peltier a presidential pardon, but backed down after two hundred FBI agents protested. Peltier was the presidential candidate of the Peace and Freedom Party in 2004. Amnesty International placed his conviction under the "Unfair Trials" category in its 2010 Annual Report.[42] In 2015, a petition was circulated online calling for his release. It is a case that will not go away. It seems now that either he will be released, in which case some Native Americans and non-Native activists will celebrate him as a hero, or he will remain in prison and be remembered by his supporters as a martyr of Wounded Knee and America's continuing racial and cultural divide. His case is important for a number of reasons, not the least of which is that it brings urgency to the otherwise sometimes abstract matter of interracial justice.

The drive for self-governance and self-determination is the unifying theme among Native Americans in the twenty-first century. At the same time, it is a theme that tends to evoke suspicion, distrust, and fear in the white community. Jacqueline Johnson, the Executive Director of the National Congress of American Indians (NCAI), spoke to these concerns in 2005: "NCAI's primary purpose is to defend tribal sovereignty at the federal level."[43] Sovereignty is simply defined as "the power of tribes to be self-determining, the power of tribes to govern their own affairs."[44] Native Americans love the vision of sovereignty. Can the mainline church embrace it? There are many reasons to give qualified, circumscribed answers to this question. Every situation is nuanced and unique. I suggest that for the church the answer will be found in how it understands and interprets the meaning of its apology to Native Americans.

Federal Policies

Over the years the policies of the federal government toward Native Americans have been inconsistent, and they remain so. On one hand, the government has taken steps to strengthen Native cultures and protect them. On the other hand, as recently as 2007 the United States was one of only four nations in the world to vote against the UN Declaration on the Rights of Indigenous People (UNDRIP). After extensive negotiations conducted at the insistence of the United States, the original document, which had been written and approved by the UN Working Group on Indigenous Populations (WGIP), was revised by the Chairperson-Rapporteur Louis Enrique Chavez without consulting with members of WGIP, and over the objections of WGIP, presented to the UN Human Rights Council. The document that President Obama signed in 2010 was the revised version of UNDRIP.[45]

Is the U.S. government bound by this diluted UNDRIP? Will disputes between tribal governments and the federal government get resolved in the UN? These are only two of the many questions awaiting future clarification. Members of the mainline church must ask if they will take a stand with Native Americans at the risk of creating new divisions in the church, or remain silent, and in their silence be complicit with the continuing exploitation and subjugation of Native peoples. What does the apology mean in this new context? That is the question with which mainline Christians must wrestle.

To his credit, President Obama brought *Cobell v. Salazar* to closure in 2009. This case originated in 1966 when Elouise Cobell, at one time the treasurer of the Blackfeet Nation, sued the federal government for its mismanagement of trust funds that had been created by the Dawes Act. The ensuing legal battle, which dragged on for forty-three years, included seven trials, ten appeals, and numerous Congressional hearings. The final settlement for $3.4 billion was at the time the largest class-action settlement in our nation's history. It provided scholarship funds for higher education, gave tribes more control over their own land, and strengthened government-to-government relations between Washington and tribal governments. Historic as this settlement was, many believe that the government still failed to honor its obligation fully. The monetary payment was much less than a full payment, and the recognition of tribal rights was equivocal. Still, the president's signature on UNDRIP and the settlement of the *Cobell v. Salazar* case portend a more just future.

The Present

Native American resistance to Anglo-colonialism is a consistent theme dating back to Powhatan resistance to the encroachments of the Virginians. Today the spirit of resistance is expressed as a unifying theme among all Native tribes as the drive for self-governance. It is clearly one of the most important issues in the twenty-first century. It has the potential to overturn the Marshall Trilogy and redefine the relationship between Native nations and the federal government. However, Native Americans remain a people under siege. The suicide rate for Native youth between the ages of fifteen and twenty-four years of age is more than three times the national average for this age group.[46] Native American reservations are often referred to as the "ultimate welfare state." The economic viability of many programs such as health care and education often depends on the government, but federal support is unreliable and programs are frequently underfunded. There are numerous lawsuits against the government and corporations pending in the courts. Those of us in the mainline church have to understand the apologies of mainline denominations to Native Americans and the repudiation of the Doctrine of Discovery in this context.

Many mainline denominations oppose the public use of symbols and logos that denigrate Native Americans. An increasing number of denominations have repudiated the Doctrine of Discovery, and some are taking steps to transfer property they hold in trust to Native communities. I believe that we are in the early stages of a new reformation. If the church comes to grips with its own history and sharpens its commitment to social justice, it will continue to evolve, and a new theological foundation will be constructed upon which the church can build a new framework for mission.

Pointing the Way

What role can and will the church play in creating a people-oriented society in the future? Two scholars, anthropologist Jack Weatherford and Andrea Smith, offer constructive proposals. Weatherford candidly notes in *Savages and Civilizations: Who Will Survive?*: "Civilization seems perfectly capable of creating its own Armageddon." To avoid such a fate, he calls upon us to remember that "we have the power to change the present and thus alter the future. The first step in that process should come by respecting the mutual right of all people to survive with dignity and to control their own destiny without surrendering their cultures."[47] The mainline church in dialogue with tribal peoples can model such a process, and in doing so offer the world a much needed alternative to violence or human rights violations.

In *Native Americans and the Christian Right: The Gendered Politics of Unlikely Alliances*, Smith writes:

To develop a mass movement that could change the current state of affairs, it is necessary to realize that the majority of the world's population (even white, middle-class men) do not benefit *in the long term* from the current social, economic and political arrangements. Most people do not have control of their lives and live at the whim of decisions made by people who they cannot even identify in the corporate world.

Then she proposes:

The key to developing a mass movement is to convince people to exchange their pursuit of short-term interests (such as maintenance of their white-skinned, economic status or gender privileges) for their long-term interests of creating a world based on social equality and justice for all.[48]

NOTES

[1]R.S. Sugirtharajah, "A Postcolonial Exploration of Collusion and Construction in Biblical Interpretation," in *The Postcolonial Bible*, ed. R.S. Sugirtharajah (Sheffield, England: Sheffield Press, 1998), 91–116.

[2]Ibid.," 104.

[3]Ibid.," 91, 94.

[4]David J. Bosch, "Vision for Mission," in *Ministry & Theology in Global Perspective: Contemporary Challenges for the Church*, ed. Don A. Pittman, Ruben L.F. Habito, and Terry C. Muck (Grand Rapids, MI: William B. Eerdmans Publishing Company, 1996), 372. Source: *International Review of Missions*, January 1987, 8–15.

[5]Rufus Anderson, *History of the Sandwich Islands: A Heathen Nation Evangelized* (Boston: Congregational Publishing Society, 1870), 11–12. Public Domain. Google digitized. Original University of Minnesota. http://babel.hathitrust.org/cgi/pt?id=umn .319510021014817;view=1up;seq=16. Accessed 12/13/15.

[6]Ojibwa, "Marriage between Indians and non-Indians," December 23, 2010. This site furnishes a report on marriages at Cornwall and a list of state laws prohibiting interracial (Native American to non-Native) marriages. http://nativeamericannetroots.net/ diary/811/marriages-between-indians-and-nonindians, italics original, 189. http:// nativeamericannetroots.net/diary/811.
Accessed 7/8/2012.

[7]David Wallace Adams, *Education for Extinction: American Indians and the Boarding School Experience 1875–1928* (Lawrence: University of Kansas Press, 1995), 6. Adams cites Robert F. Berkhofer, Jr., *The White Man's Indians: Images of the American Indian from Columbus to the Present* (New York: Alfred A. Knopf, 1978), 134–35. For Jefferson's statement see Paul L. Ford, ed., *The Writings of Thomas* Jefferson (New York: G. P. Putnam's Sons, 1892). For both citations see fn 4 on 340.

[8]Ibid., 6. The House Committee Report is quoted by Alice C. Fletcher, *Indian Education and Civilization*, Senate Exec. Doc. No 95, 48th Cong., 2nd. Sess., 1888, serial 2542, 162–63. See Adams, fn 5 on 340.

[9]Howard Zinn, *A People's History of the United States: 1492–Present* (New York: HarperPerennial edition, 1995), 146.

[10]See Robert A. Williams, Jr. "Indian Rights and the Marshall Court," in *Like a Loaded Weapon: The Rehnquist Court, Indian Rights, and the Legal History of Racism in America* (Minneapolis: University of Minnesota Press, 2005), 47–70.

[11]Ibid., 48.

[12]Ward Churchill, *Struggle for the Land: Indigenous Resistance to Genocide, Ecocide and Expropriation in Contemporary North America* (Monroe, ME: Common Courage Press, 1993) discusses the Doctrine of Discovery and the Right of Conquest, 35–36.

[13]Williams, *Loaded Weapon*, 49.

[14]Ibid., 56.

[15]Ibid., 56.

[16]*Johnson & Graham Lessee v. McIntosh*, 21 U.S. 8 Wheat. 543 543 (1823). https://supreme.justia.com/cases/federal/us/21/543/case.html.

[17]Vine Deloria, Jr., "The Application of the Constitution to American Indians," in *Exiles*, italics added by Deloria, *Johnson v. McIntosh*, 299.

[18]*Cherokee Nation v. State of Georgia*, 1831. https://www.mtholyoke.edu/acad/intrel/cherokee.htm. Accessed 6/6/2014.

[19]*Cherokee Nation v. Georgia.* www.law.cornell.edu/supremecourt/text//30/1. Accessed 6/6/2014.

[20]Cherokee National Cultural Resource Center, "Samuel Worcester," www.cherokee.org/AboutTheNation/History/Biographies/SamuelWorcester.aspx. Accessed 6/22/2014.

[21]Williams, *Loaded Weapon*, 70.

[22]George E. Tinker, *Missionary Conquest: The Gospel and Native American Cultural Genocide* (Minneapolis: Fortress Press, 1993),19.

[23]Francis Paul Prucha, *The Churches and the Indian Schools 1888–1912* (Lincoln: University of Nebraska Press, 1979), 1. Prucha notes that the Bureau of Catholic Indian Missions was established in 1879. As the Catholic population in the United States grew, the Catholic Church stepped up its mission work. Prucha documents the competition between the Board of Indian Commissioners and the Bureau of Catholic Indian Missions for the control and education of Native children. The federal government agreed to pay each agency an annual amount for each student enrolled. Hence, the number of students enrolled had financial consequences.

[24]Ulysses S. Grant, First Annual Message, 1869, in Richardson, ed., *Papers of the Presidents*, vol. 9, 3993. Cited by Ronald Takaki, *A Different Mirror: A History of Multicultural America*, rev. ed. (Boston: Back Bay Books, 2008), 94. See fn 45 on 462.

[25]Stephen Cornell, Joseph P. Kalt, et al., *The State of Native Nations: Conditions under U.S. Policies of Self-Determination* (New York: Oxford University Press, 2008), 200.

[26]Adams, *Education for Extinction*, 27.

[27]Board of Indian Commissioners, "Indian Education," from the Twelfth Annual Report of the Board of Indian Commissioners (1880), in *Americanizing the American Indians: Writings by 'Friends of the Indians' 1880–1900, 7–9*, ed. Francis Prucha (Cambridge, MA: Harvard University Press, 1973), 193–94.

[28]Thomas Morgan, "Compulsory Education," from the proceedings of the Tenth Annual Meeting of the Lake Mohonk Conference of Friends of the Indians (1892), 51–54, in *Americanizing*, ed. Prucha, 252.

[29]Lyman Abbot, "Education for the Indian," from the Proceedings of the Sixth Annual Meeting of the Lake Mohonk Conference of Friends of the Indians (1888), 11–16, *Americanizing*, ed. Prucha, 209.

[30]Adams, *Education for Extinction*, explains the start of off-reservation schools and Henry Pratt's roll, 36–51.

[31]Ibid., 55. Adams cites Richard Henry Pratt, *Battlefield and Classroom: Four Decades with the American Indian 1867–1904*, ed. Robert M. Utley (New Haven, CT: Yale University Press, 1964), 283.

[32]Source: Barbara Landis, "Carlisle Indian Industrial School History," copyright 1966, Barbara Landis. http://home.epix.net/~landis/histry.html.

[33]Henry Pratt, "The Advantages of Mingling Indians with Whites," in *Americanizing*, ed. Prucha, 261, 269.

[34]George Tinker, *American Indian Liberation: A Theology of Sovereignty*, (Maryknoll, NY: Orbis Books, 2008), 22.

[35]Alice Fletcher, "The Dawes Act 1887," http://www.nebraskastudies.org/0600/frameset_reset.html?http://www. nebraskastudies.org/0600/stories/0601_0200.html. Accessed 6/25/2014.

[36]Henry L. Dawes, "Defense of the Dawes Act," in *Americanizing*, ed. Prucha, 101.

[37]Cornell, Kalt, et al., *Native Nations*, 4.

[38]Julie Davis, "American Indian Boarding School Experiences," *OAH Magazine of History*, vol. 15, no. 2. Desegregation (Winter, 2001): 20–22. http://www.jstor.org/ stable/25163421. Accessed: 6/9/2014.

[39]W. Roger Buffalohead, "The Indian New Deal: A Review Essay," *Minnesota History Magazine*, vol.48, no. 8 (Winter 1983), 339–41. http://www.jstor.org/stable/20178854. Accessed 6/15/2014.

[40]John Collier, "We Took Away Their Best Lands, Broke Treaties," http:// historymatters.gmu.edu/d/5058/. Accessed 6/14/2014.

[41]Tinker, *Liberation*, 22.

[42]Amnesty International, *Annual Report: USA 2010*, May 28, 2010. www.amnestyusa. org/research/reports/annual-report-usa-2010?page=4. Accessed 1/11/2015.

[43]Jacqueline Johnson (Tlingit), "Defending Tribal Sovereignty," in Cornell, Kalt, et al., *Native Nations*, 374.

[44]Ibid., 373.

[45]Charmaine White Face, Ogala Tetuwan, Spokesperson for the Sioux Nation Treaty Council, kindly provided me with "An Analysis of the Declaration on the Rights of Indigenous Peoples," August, 2010 (unpublished). She reports that the Sioux Nation Treaty Council was involved in the development of the Declaration beginning in 1984. Indigenous people from throughout the world contributed to the development of this document. This Declaration was approved by the UN Sub-Commission on the Prevention of Discrimination and Protection of Minorities (now called the Sub-Committee on the Promotion and Protection of Human Rights) and the UN Working Group on Indigenous Populations in 1994. The changes consistently weakened the demands and undermine the rights of Indigenous peoples, as the following example illustrates. Paragraph 10 in the original text begins: *Emphasizing* the need for demilitarization of the lands and territories of indigenous peoples.... In the General Assembly approved document this paragraph beings: "*Emphasizing* the contribution of the demilitarization of the lands and territories of indigenous peoples....Removing the words "need for" and inserting the words "contribution to" changes the whole meaning of the paragraph. After the change in wording the paragraph ceases to address the present or future situations.

[46]Laurie Meyers, "A Struggle for Hope," *Monitor on Psychology*, vol. 38, no. 2, Feb. 2007, 30.

www.apa.org/monitor//feb07/astruggle.aspx. Accessed 3/22/2014.

[47]Jack Weatherford, *Savages and Civilizations: Who Will Survive?* (New York: Fawcett Columbine, 1994), 289, 290.

[48]Andrea Smith, *Native Americans and the Christian Right: The Gendered Politics of Unlikely Alliances* (Durham, NC: Duke University Press, 2008), italics original, 252, 253.

PART THREE

Responsibility

We have dug into our past and unearthed and recognized some of the root causes of Christian anti–Native attitudes. Thus, we have completed the first leg of our journey from Jamestown to Justicetown. Now we have to accept responsibility for healing the resulting wounds. In chapters six and seven I examine the theological paradigm that informed the mission to "civilize and Christianize the Indians." In chapter eight, I draw comparisons between the apology of the mainline church to Native Americans in the United States and the apology of the United Church of Canada to First Nations peoples as each ecclesiastical body accepts responsibility for its past. Chapters nine and ten anticipate a more just and peaceful future for all people as we learn what it means to act in deep solidarity with one another.

I want to pause here and reiterate two observations. First, the apologies of the mainline denominations signal that members of the church have awakened to the pain they have inflicted on indigenous peoples. The last five hundred years of U.S. history may justly be labeled a period of religious persecution. Getting in touch with this history is perhaps the only way to overcome the colonial mentality and spirituality that still inhabits the church. Liberation theologian Gustavo Gutierrez tells us that "overcoming the colonial mentality is one of the most important tasks of the Christian community."[1] This is our task.

My second observation is that taking responsibility means being accountable. In words attributed to Jesus, we must "take the log out of our own eye" (Mt. 7:5), with the "log" here being the narrative about itself and about Native Americans that the church shaped, told, and embraced. This story gave the church strength and confidence as it sent missionaries forth to "civilize and Christianize the Indians." We must free ourselves from this narrative and from embedded assumptions of entitlement, superiority, and white privilege to create a new narrative fit for the future.

NOTE

[1]Gustavo Gutierrez, *A Theology of Liberation: History, Politics and Salvation.* Trans. and ed. by Sister Caridad Inda and John Eagleson (Maryknoll, NY: Orbis Books, 1973), 140.

6

Christianity at a Crossroads

The mainline church is at a crossroads. Either it will continue on the road to Justicetown—my metaphor for a future in which treaty obligations with Native Americans are honored, their civil rights restored, and their right to self-governance recognized—or it will return to the (dis)comfort of the status quo, in which case liberal Christians who mean well and who sincerely want to be reconciled with Native Americans will for various reasons be unable or unwilling to stand in deep solidarity with them. The question before the church is whether we are prepared to pay the price of costly discipleship. So this is a defining moment for the church. We must indeed lose our life in order to find it (Mt. 10:39). This is the way of the cross.

In practical terms, losing our life means decoding the cultural creed that legitimized the mission to Christianize Native peoples. As white, relatively prosperous members of the mainline church, we have to ask ourselves how we discern the presence of God as something other than the extension of our own power. To borrow a phrase from *The Predicament of the Prosperous* by Bruce C. Birch and Larry R. Rasmussen, the call to responsibility is a "God-wrestle" akin to Jacob's "God-wrestle" (Gen. 32).[1] It is a story of pain and transformation, but also of hope for Jacob as he comes to terms with his brother Esau, whom he has cheated and from whom he is estranged. In the course of the nighttime struggle, Jacob comes to realize that destiny is not in his control. The conquest of his image of self-sufficiency forces him to acquire a new identity that allows for deep solidarity.

The Exodus story was the creedal story of the English who settled Jamestown. They believed that England had inherited the mantle of Jews and that they were God's chosen people. When the Pilgrims and Puritans came to New England, they believed that they were on an "errand in the wilderness." They likened their journey crossing the Atlantic Ocean to Moses's parting of the Red Sea. America was their "Promised Land." By the time of the Revolutionary War, colonial rebels pictured the American colonies as "God's New Israel." Over time, Birch

71

and Rasmussen contend, "The themes of deliverance rooted in Exodus have become totally entwined in the American success story."[2]

Bruce Feiler proposes in *America's Prophet: Moses and the American Story* that Moses is our nation's "true founding father."[3] He suggests that in spite of past mistreatment of blacks, Native Americans, immigrants, women, and gays, the Exodus tradition perpetuates "the idea that the strength of a society comes from its ability to protect its entire population and provide everyone with a path out of pain into promise."[4] The Exodus narrative, as interpreted in our national mythology, is a story of individual freedom and equality, which are bedrock values of our culture.

Now in the postapology era, the church needs to deconstruct our prevalent understanding of the Exodus story and reinterpret it as a story of liberation *and* conquest. The liberation story is well-rehearsed in the "land of the free and the home of the brave." The conquest story is less well-known outside tribal communities. It is time that we hear the voices of indigenous peoples.

Defining Our Identity Story

The late Marcus Borg, an influential religious scholar and interpreter of scripture in the mainline church, calls the Exodus Israel's "story of sacred origins....It not only told the story of Israel's creation but shaped the world in which she lived."[5] Memory of the Exodus continues to shape Jewish identity. This story of the flight to freedom is retold annually in the celebration of Passover during which Jews remember the events surrounding the journey to freedom and claim this ancient story as their own. Many mainline Christian congregations enact a symbolic Seder meal during the Christian holy season of Lent. Participating congregations recount Israel's dramatic flight to freedom as they eat bitter herbs and other foods, and in so doing make Israel's birth story part of their own narrative.

Borg identifies the Exodus as Israel's "primal narrative," by "primal" meaning that it is Israel's most important story, its story of origins, and its archetypal story, the story that "narrates the perennial struggle between the world of empire and the liberating will of God, between the lordship of Pharaoh and the lordship of God."[6] He points out that the exodus is fundamentally a story of promise and fulfillment that has two main parts: conquest of the land of Canaan and the promise of a multitude of generations. The third part is a series of specific threats to the promise.

The drama begins to unfold when God promises Abraham and Sarah: "Go from your country and your kindred and your father's house to the land that I will show you. And I will make you a great nation" (Gen. 12:1–2a). We soon learn that Israel's matriarchs—Sarah, Rebekah, and Rachel—are barren women whose inability to bear children puts the future of Israel at risk. Although there is no virgin birth in these stories, time and again God faithfully intervenes to keep alive the promise of a multitude of generations.

A new threat to the promise looms when the sons of Jacob (the grandson of Abraham and the son of Isaac) sell their brother Joseph to human traffickers who take him to Egypt. After numerous trials, Joseph establishes himself in a key post in the pharaoh's government. When famine in the land of Israel drives Joseph's brothers to Egypt in hopes of finding food, Joseph is there to welcome them. The brothers' betrayal is turned into a life-saving blessing.

The Hebrew people settle in Egypt and prosper. Their population grows. The pharaoh sees what is happening and becomes concerned that the Hebrews are too numerous. In order to control them, he enslaves them. Through this long series of events, the pattern of promise-threat-fulfillment is firmly established, and we are ready for Israel's flight to freedom, which Marcus Borg identifies as "a paradigmatic story of God's character and will," and "Israel's decisive and constitutive 'identity story,'"[7] which unfolds in four episodes: (1) deliverance, (2) rebellion, (3) subjugation, and (4) conquest of the Promised Land.

Deliverance

The story of Israel's deliverance begins with groans of hope rising from the lips of oppressed Hebrew slaves. The deep sighs and anguished cries of this marginalized community reach the ears of God, who is moved by their plea to come to their rescue. Yahweh tells his servant Moses, who grew up in pharaoh's house but later became a fugitive from pharaoh's justice:

> I have seen the affliction of my people who are in Egypt, and have heard their cry because of their taskmaster; I know their sufferings, and I have come down to deliver them out of the hand of the Egyptians, and to bring them up out of that land to a good and broad land, a land flowing with milk and honey, to the place of the Canaanites.…Come, I will send you to Pharaoh that you may bring forth my people, the sons of Israel, out of Egypt (Ex. 3:7–8, 10).

God promises to liberate Israel "with an outstretched arm and with great acts of judgment" (Ex. 6:6). Using supernatural power, God rains down destruction and death upon the Egyptians (whose hearts God has hardened) until at last Moses leads the people across the Red Sea into the wilderness and freedom. The first act of the freedom drama is completed.

Rebellion

In the second act of this drama, the liberated slaves follow Moses into the desert where God guides them with a pillar of cloud by day and a column of fire by night. Even here, threats to Israel's survival are present. But in the desert wilderness, God faithfully quenches the people's thirst with water from a rock and mercifully satisfies their hunger with heaven-sent manna and quail. Finally the fugitives arrive at Sinai, where a new chapter in the formation of their identity begins.

Borg notes that "what happens at Sinai is that Israel becomes a people, a nation." "It is here that Israel comes into existence."[8] As the curtain rises on the second act, we learn that

> Moses went up to God, and the Lord called him out of the mountain, saying, "Thus you shall say to the house of Jacob, and tell the people of Israel: You have seen what I did to the Egyptians, and how I bore you on eagles' wings and brought you to myself. Now therefore, if you obey my voice and keep my covenant, you shall be my own possession among all peoples; for the earth is mine, and you shall be to me a kingdom of priests and a holy nation (Ex. 19:3–5).

When the meeting is over, Moses descends from the mountain and speaks to the waiting people. He gives them the Ten Commandments, the Book of the Covenant and a series of cultic, civil, and criminal laws and basic ethical norms. These law and norms are intended to make Israel a new kind of society—a society that is the antithesis of the pharaoh-dominated world they left behind. Most important, this scene introduces the roles of Moses as mediator of Israel's covenant with Yahweh and bearer of divine law.

There are a number of noteworthy features of the covenant. First, God initiates and sustains the covenant. Second, the covenant is drawn from the life of the people. Two of the most striking laws establish the sabbath year and the jubilee year. Every sabbath (seventh) year, debts owed by Israelites to other Israelites are to be forgiven and slaves are to be set free. Every jubilee (fiftieth) year, lands are to be returned to the original families of ownership. The purpose of these laws is to prevent a return to Egypt-like conditions of oppression and marginalization and to maintain a certain level of economic equality and political freedom.

Richard Horsley, the author of twenty books on the Bible, points out in his study of Israel as a covenant society that "the most striking feature of the Covenant is that it establishes a relationship between the people and Yahweh that is inseparably political-economic and (almost by definition) religious....When Yahweh delivers the Hebrews from bondage in Egypt it is a political liberation from subjection but also an economic emancipation from such servitude."[9] The sabbath year and the jubilee year codify this history.

A third feature of the covenant is that the people's prime motivation for keeping the law is gratitude. God the liberator makes it possible for the people to live in a very different kind of society—a society in which people are free from perpetual servitude. Fourth, Israel's proper response to the covenant is obedience. Fifth, the covenant establishes an exclusive relationship between God and Israel, and this relationship is the foundation of their society. The message is clear, "You shall have no other gods before me....For I the Lord your God am a jealous God" (Ex. 20:3, 5). The God of the covenant is Israel's God, and Israel's identity is as the people of God.

Once the covenant is ratified, the Israelites are a people of the covenant. They have a clear and distinct identity and a firm foundation. But even in this new context, the overarching pattern of promise and fulfillment with accompanying threats endures. The new identity requires new patterns of behavior, but these patterns are not yet fully engrained in the lives of the people. It is not surprising that the two most immediate threats to Israel's new identity come from within the community itself.

The first threat, which comes in the form of economic anarchy, challenges Moses's role as covenant mediator. The second threat, which comes in the form of political anarchy, challenges Moses's role as lawgiver. If Moses cannot successfully meet these threats and solidly establish his leadership role, God's experiment will fail, and Israel will sink into a sea of chaos instead of emerging as a model covenant community.

The economic threat is capsulized in the well-known story of the golden calf, found in Exodus 32. The prolonged absence of Moses creates anxiety in the minds of the people and causes them to become concerned for their safety. Looking for some tangible reassurance of God's presence and favor, they turn to Aaron and demand: "Up, make us gods, who shall go before us; as for this Moses, the man who brought us up out of the land of Egypt, we do not know what has become of him" (Ex. 32:1).

Under Aaron's direction, the people melt their jewelry and make a golden calf, which eases the people's anxiety but violates their covenant with Yahweh and poses a new threat to their survival. The disobedience of the people kindles Yahweh's anger against them. God calls them "corrupt" (Ex. 32:7) and "a stiff-necked people" (Ex. 32:9). Yahweh instructs his servant Moses: "Let me alone, that my wrath may burn hot against them and I may consume them; but of you I will make a great nation" (Ex. 32:10).

Moses responds to God's command with an intercession on behalf of the people. He pleads: "Turn from thy fierce wrath, and repent of this evil against thy people" (Ex. 32:12b). And he challenges the Lord of Hosts to "Remember Abraham, Isaac, and Israel, thy servants, to whom thou didst swear by thine own self...'I will multiply your descendants...and all this land that I have promised I will give to your descendants, and they shall inherit it forever.'" (Ex. 32:13). Moses's successful intervention confirms his role as covenant mediator.

No sooner is Moses's role as covenant mediator confirmed than his role as law-giver is tested. The author of the book of Exodus reports that "Moses saw that the people had broken loose" (Ex. 32:25). What exactly "broken loose" means is not clear, but we may assume that they are breaking loose from some aspect of the law. In the next sentence we learn that "Moses stood at the gate of the camp and said, 'Who is on the Lord's side? Come to me.' And all the sons of Levi gathered themselves to him" (Ex. 32:26).

Subjugation

Whether this summons marks the beginning of the priesthood is uncertain, but Moses's instructions to the sons of Levi and the consequences are very clear:

> Thus says the Lord God of Israel, "Put every man his sword on his side, and go to and fro from gate to gate throughout the camp, and slay every man his brother, and every man his companion, and every man his neighbor." And the sons of Levi did according to the word of Moses; and there fell of the people that day about three thousand men (Ex. 32:27–28).

Once the mission is accomplished, Moses tells the sons of Levi: "Today you have ordained yourselves for the service of the Lord, each one at the cost of his son and of his brother, that he may bestow a blessing upon you this day" (Ex. 32:29). It is this event that secures Moses's role as the giver and the enforcer of the law.

Much as the English war upon the Irish prefigured the English invasion of America, this event in the wilderness presaged the Hebrew conquest of Canaan. The English brought with them to the New World the lessons learned in their war upon the Irish. In the same way, when the Hebrew people entered the Promised Land, they brought with them the lesson of obedience that they had learned in the wilderness. But there is an important qualification. In the wilderness, the Levites were killing their kindred, and for this reason the slaughter was limited. When they entered the Promised Land, there were no restrictions.

Moses, the unquestioned spiritual and political leader of Israel, now receives a new set of instructions and a new promise. God tells him, "Depart....And I will send an angel before you, and I will drive out the Canaanites, the Amorites, the Hittites, the Perizzites, the Hivites, and the Jebusites" (Ex. 33:2).

Conquest of the Promised Land

The overarching pattern of promise and fulfillment with attending threats continues after the people leave Sinai. Moses dies before Israel can enter the Promised Land. But God remains faithful to the covenant. In the fourth act of the drama, God calls Joshua to the position of leadership. As Joshua prepares for the days to come, God assures him: "Be strong and of good courage; for you shall cause this people to inherit the land which I swore to their fathers to give them." (Josh. 1:6).

Borg concludes: "The exodus story is about the creation of a world marked by freedom, social justice, and *shalom*, a rich Hebrew word meaning well-being, peace, and wholeness." He assures us: "Both the exodus story and the theme of promise and fulfillment were strikingly relevant to the situation of the Jewish people in the exilic postexilic periods....Indeed, the theme of promise and fulfillment is strikingly relevant to people in *all* times....When birth and rebirth seem impossible, when pharaohs and the powers of empires seem to rule the world, God's faithfulness can be counted on."[10]

So interpreted, the Exodus is a powerful and deeply satisfying story of persistent hope and undaunted courage. It is a story of triumph against all odds. It is the assurance that if the people of the covenant remain faithful to the covenant in precarious times, God will faithfully fulfill promises made in the covenant. This is the well-rehearsed identity story. But it is not a story that we can accept uncritically in a postapology world. The Exodus narrative as it has been traditionally interpreted cannot be a primary narrative for the Christian church in a postapology age. Reinventing the mainline church means nothing less than creating a new identity story.

Decoding Our Identity Story

Robert Allen Warrior, a member of the Osage Nation, calls upon white Christians to read the Exodus story from the underside—to read with "Canaanite eyes." In "Native American Perspective: Canaanites, Cowboys, and Indians," Warrior contends that "the Exodus is an inappropriate way for Native Americans to think about liberation," yet "where discussion about Christian involvement in Native American activism must begin."[11]

When we read the Exodus account from below, from the perspective of the Canaanites, this story of promise and fulfillment becomes a story of destruction and death. Warrior insists that for indigenous peoples "Yahweh the deliverer became Yahweh the conqueror."[12] The God who pledged to Moses, "I will bring you into a land which I swore to give to Abraham, to Isaac, and to Jacob; I will give it to you for a possession. I am the Lord" (Ex. 6:8), instructed the Israelites as follows:

> When the Lord your God brings you into the land which you are entering to take possession of it, and clears away many nations before your, the Hittites, the Girgashites, the Amorites, the Canaanites, the Perizzites, and Hivites and the Jebusites, seven nations greater and mightier than yourselves, and when the Lord your God gives them over to you, and you defeat them; then you must utterly destroy them; you shall make no covenant with them, and show no mercy to them (Deut. 7:1–2).

God is now declaring unconditional war upon the indigenous inhabitants of Canaan. The decimation in the wilderness is about to be repeated on a much grander scale. Indigenous genocide is the order of the day.

In the wilderness, Israelites were killing other Israelites—brother against brother, father against son, neighbor against neighbor. Terrible as it was, the slaughter was limited and purposeful. The death of three thousand confirmed Moses's role as Israel's political leader and established discipline in the ranks of the faithful. Faith became associated with obedience. In contrast, the Canaanites were completely external to the Israelites. Their presence posed a threat to the identity of the Israelites as a covenant people. They could be annihilated. Indeed, they had to be destroyed. Warrior says: "One of the most important of Yahweh's commandments is the prohibition on social relations with Canaanites or participation in their religion."[13] This prohibition was used by the Israelites to justify Canaanite genocide. Thus Israel's theology of liberation for the slave became a theology of death for the native.

Warrior challenges indigenous people to ask themselves if they can trust the God of the Judeo-Christian tradition. Can they trust the church that the late Floyd Crow Westerman, a renowned Sioux musician, activist, and actor, described as an "ever circling vulture" descending on its prey to "pick the soul to pieces"?[14] Reading the Exodus story with Canaanite eyes, it is hard to see how this story can become a path out of pain for indigenous peoples. This is not to deny that many Native Americans self-identify as Christian, but white Christians for whom the Exodus tradition has been an identity story must neither assume Native Americans share the same interpretation of this tradition nor continue to interpret the Exodus narrative in a one-sided way as a story of freedom. Exodus is a story of liberation *and* conquest. The discussion within Native communities about the Exodus story may offer hope that we who are white, Christian, and members of the mainline church can learn to interpret the Exodus story from below. But it may also mean that we need to find a new identity story that is fit for the quest for interracial justice with Native Americans.

Warrior offers a number of steps that white Anglo-Saxon Protestant Christians who value the mainline church can take as we revisit this birth-story of liberation that is now also a story of conquest and death.[15] First, he asserts, we must put indigenous peoples at the center of Christian theological reflection and political action. The story of conquest has to be taken seriously. It is a violent story. This "text of terror," to borrow Phyllis Trible's descriptive phrase, "refutes all claims to the superiority of a Christian era."[16] Turning around the charge of barbarism that white Christians have so often leveled against Native Americans, Warrior says: "It is to those who believe in these texts that the barbarism belongs. It is those who act on the basis of these texts who must take responsibility for the terror and violence they can and have engendered."[17] We must accept the reality that well-meaning missionaries who came to bring civilization and the gospel to indigenous peoples committed barbaric acts, and we must be chastened by this knowledge.

Second, Warrior urges us to become more aware of how themes of conquest have become part of our national consciousness and ideology. He encourages us to study the works of Puritan preachers who referred to Natives as Canaanites—people worthy of annihilation. Preachers like Increase Mather and his son Cotton Mather used the language of "chosen people" to justify domination and genocide. White Anglo-Saxon Protestants in the mainline church must take responsibility for this history, examine our language and metaphors, and disarm our theology.

Third, Warrior asks of the entire Exodus story: "Is it appropriate to the needs of indigenous people seeking justice and deliverance?" Of the God who commanded the slaughter of the natives, he asks, "Do Native Americans and other indigenous people dare trust the same god in their struggle for justice?"[18] Answering his own question, Warrior declares:

> We, the wretched of the earth, may be well advised this time
> not to listen to outsiders with their promises of liberation and
> deliverance. We will perhaps do better to look elsewhere for
> our vision of justice, peace, and political sanity—and vision
> through which we escape not only our oppressors, but our
> oppression as well. Maybe, for once, we will just have to listen
> to ourselves, leaving the gods of this continent's real strangers
> to do battle among themselves.[19]

The Israelite's vision of the Canaanite's homeland as a territory divinely ordained for their use blinded them to the humanity of its inhabitants, who, according to the text, were completely expendable. Warrior suggests that Native people cannot find solace in this story. It offers them neither a path out of pain nor hope for the future. Likewise, I now believe that a church that for centuries relied upon this narrative to justify its participation in Native American genocide cannot now find in this same story a vision of interracial justice.

The conquest of the Promised Land is not a vision of *shalom*. Warrior calls indigenous people to look to their own native traditions for a vision of justice, peace, and political sanity. We who are members of the mainline church likewise must look to our own traditions and either rehabilitate Christian concepts in ways that will lead us out of the colonial mess we are in today or find a new paradigm.[20] I believe that the call to read the Exodus story from below means that we must move from dogmatic certitude to creative dialogue.

From Dogma to Dialogue

The difficulty of Warrior's call for the mainline church to put indigenous peoples at the center of its theology is illustrated in William Stolzman's *The Pipe and the Cross: A Christian-Sioux Dialogue*.[21] The book is based on a series of biweekly Monday conversations between Lakota medicine men, most of whom came from the Rosebud Reservation, and Christian pastors, most of whom were Catholic. The meetings took place over a period of six years, from 1973 to 1979. Stolzman, a Jesuit pastor, was a missionary to the Rosebud Reservation and chairman of the Medicine Men and Pastors' Meetings. During these meetings, participants examined the meaning of sacred Lakota and Christian stories, symbols, rituals, and ceremonies.

Stolzman tells us that these meetings were "directed toward mutual understanding and respect for the Lakota and Christian religions" and were intended to "help individuals understand and appreciate the Lakota religion and how it can be related to the Christian religion."[22] The process was a "thick" multilayered conversation. All of the meetings were conducted in both Lakota and English. Time was taken to explain, explore, and examine Lakota and Christian stories, symbols, rituals, and ceremonies to ensure that all the participants felt that they had been heard and that their opinions, differences, and similarities were respected.

The process was consistent with the avowed purpose of helping all participants gain mutual understanding and respect for the Lakota and Christian traditions as these traditions were understood by the participants. Members of the meetings understood that they were speaking for themselves and that there were people outside the meetings who were openly critical of what they were doing.

I admire members of the Medicine Men and Pastors' Meetings circle for their care for each other and their candor. Prolonged and intentional encounters are necessary if we want to move from doctrinal debates to dialogue. However, the second purpose of the meetings seems to run counter to the first purpose. That is, the intent of helping people understand how Lakota religion related to Christian religion implies the Christian tradition is normative, as Stolzman's conclusion suggests: "While the Christian religion welcomes pre-Christian enrichments, the Lakota religion does not welcome them." He adds that both traditions must be grounded in "respect of the Unity of God."[23] Lastly, he approves of "practicing Lakota religion in the Lakota community," and of "practicing the Christian religion in the context of universal needs unto eternal salvation."[24] These statements imply a spiritual evolution from religion that responds to the particularity of the Lakota community to the Christian religion which, in Stolzman's words, addresses "universal needs unto eternal salvation." This is a particularly Christian way of interpreting an interfaith dialogue.

To borrow a phrase from Kwok Pui-lan, a Chinese biblical scholar and postcolonial theologian, we have yet to learn how to "read the Bible in a non-biblical world."[25] An examination of postcolonial methods of biblical study would take us too far afield from the purpose of this investigation. But we can draw on the insights of some scholars in the field to establish some parameters and general rules.[26]

First, in a multicultural world, we must approach claims to biblical authority with caution and more than a little suspicion born of our knowledge of past historical abuses and misuses of the Bible. The Bible was and still is for many people a text of terror. Christian people have committed and still commit barbarous acts. Second, we must be aware of our social location, by which I mean the communities to which we belong, the processes we are using to select and interpret certain texts that comprise our primary narrative, the consequences of our choices, and the ways that our choices may project and protect white privilege and power. Third, we must guard against what I call a reverse binary, making the assumption that God has "gone native."

The missionaries of the past were convinced that their mission was to "civilize and Christianize Indians." In this postapology era white Christians tend to assume that nothing good can come from Christianity and that God is on the side of the Natives. Our beginning place, I suggest, is a concern for the well-being of people. We have to wrestle with sometimes conflicting ideas of what constitutes an ethical and good society. This concern identifies a borderland where indigenous peoples and nonnatives can meet and negotiate their differences as we look for common ground.

NOTES

[1]Bruce C. Birch and Larry R. Rasmussen, *The Predicament of the Prosperous* (Philadelphia: Westminster Press, 1978), 74–75.

[2]Ibid., 95.

[3]Bruce Feiler, *America's Prophet: Moses and the American Story* (New York: HarperCollins, Publishers, 2009), 66.

[4]Ibid., 302.

[5]Marcus J. Borg, *Reading the Bible Again for the First Time: Taking the Bible Seriously but Not Literally* (New York: HarperCollins Publishers, Inc., 2001), 86.

[6]Ibid., 92, 93.

[7]Ibid., 103.

[8]Ibid., 99.

[9]Richard A. Horsley, *Covenant Economics: A Biblical Vision of Justice for All* (Louisville, KY: Westminster John Knox Press, 2000), 23.

[10]Borg, *Reading*, italics original, 105,106.

[11]Robert Allen Warrior, "A Native American Perspective: Canaanites, Cowboys, and Indians," in *Voices from the Margin: Interpreting the Bible in the Third World*, ed. R. S. Sugirtharajah (Maryknoll, NY: Orbis Books, 1997). Warrior's essay first appeared in *Christianity and Crisis*, 49 (12, 1989), 278, 282.

[12]Ibid., 279.

[13]Ibid., 281.

[14]Floyd Red Crow Westerman, "Missionaries," Copyright 2000–2012, Lyrics Archive. http://www.thelyricarchive.com/song/1606667-209398/Missionaries. Accessed 12/13/2015.

[15]Warrior, "A Native American Perspective," 283–85.

[16]Phyllis Trible, *Texts of Terror: Literary-Feminist Readings of Biblical Narratives* (Philadelphia: Fortress Press, 1984), 2.

[17]Warrior, "A Native American Perspective," 283.

[18]Ibid., 284.

[19]Ibid., 285.

[20]Fernando F. Segovia and R.S. Sugirtharajah, eds., *A Postcolonial Commentary on the New Testament* (London: Clark, 2007) and R. S. Sugirtharajah, ed., *The Postcolonial Bible* (Sheffield, Eng.: Sheffield Academic Press, 1998).

[21]William Stolzman, *The Pipe and the Cross: A Christian-Sioux Dialogue* (Chamberlain, SD: Tipi Press, 2002).

[22]Ibid., 13.

[23]Ibid., 210.

[24]Ibid., 218.

[25]Kwok Pui-lan, "Discovering the Bible in a Non-Biblical World," 289–305. The article is a reprint from *Semeia* 47 (1989).

[26] Fernando F. Segovia and Mary Ann Tolbert, eds. *Teaching the Bible: The Discourses and Politics of Biblical Pedagogy* (Maryknoll, NY: Orbis Books, 1998).

7

Images of God and Our Social Order

Putting indigenous peoples at the center of white theology and engaging with indigenous peoples as dialogue partners in a search for wisdom means that we have to deconstruct conventional metaphysical monotheism—the theological framework of colonial Christianity. Only after we decolonize our minds can we enter into the constructive task of seeking a theological pathway that leads us away from conquest and toward interracial justice.

Deconstructing Monotheism

Laurel Schneider, a member of the faculty of Chicago Theological Seminary, shows us in *Beyond Monotheism* that while the concept of one, universal ruling deity has great antiquity, the word "monotheism" is surprisingly modern.[1] It does not appear in publications until 1680, about fifty years after the terms "polytheist" and "polytheism" appeared. She suggests that the word was first used as a polemical tool either to defend Christianity against other religions or to discredit Jews. In either case, monotheism was conceived of as a "classifying enterprise."[2] She contends that as a classifying enterprise, the monotheism-polytheism binary is ultimately reductionist on two counts. First, it discounts nontheistic religions. Second, it implies a theory of evolution from the many to the one. Let us consider each of these tendencies of monotheism in turn.

The word "theism" refers to a being (or beings) who is person-like and divine. Divinity has to be understood in this fashion. Given this assumption, all nontheistic religious claims are not legitimate. The conflict between English rectors and Powhatan priests discussed earlier in this book illustrates the confusion created when theistic and nontheistic faith traditions collide. The traditions of the former centered on the worship of an abstract deity, sin and grace, life and death. The traditions of the latter were attuned to the patterns and elements of nature and encouraged living in harmony with nature. The English

Virginian's theistic frame of reference simply could not accommodate the Powhatan worldview, nor could the Powhatans comprehend the Christian theology of the English Virginians. There was no pathway to dialogue.

A second problem with the monotheism-polytheism binary is that it has within it an evolutionary tendency. Schneider cites as an example of this bias David Hume's defense of "rational religion." In 1757 Hume argued:

> If we consider the improvement of human society from rude beginnings to a state of greater perfection, polytheism or idolatry was, and necessarily must have been, the first and most ancient of mankind.[3]

The 1893 World Parliament of Religions, which displayed a model of the primitive conditions of mock Native American villages and contrasted their "pitiful condition" with a more advanced level of civilization and a monotheistic religion, brought Hume's argument to life.

As noted in the discussion of the Exodus narrative found in the previous chapter, Israelites became a covenant people at Sinai. There they learned that their God was a jealous God. They could have no other gods before God. There was one God. What Moses and the people of Israel came to understand in the wilderness is that there is a nonnegotiable order of reality governed by Yahweh—a jealous lawgiver who demanded and rewarded fidelity and obedience. Conversely, Yahweh promised to punish and if need be to destroy the disobedient and the ignorant.

An enduring lesson that people of faith have taken from the Sinai covenant is that in God's realm, obedience and our well-being are tightly linked together. Disobedience leads to ruination or annihilation. Therefore, obedience to the law is not mere legalism but conforming to the very structure of reality established and governed by an omnipotent and omniscient God.

Critics of this type of revealed religion argue that it creates a top-down theology that is vulnerable to imperial politics. The people who are disobedient or just plain ignorant are Other. Frantz Fanon says that by definition the Other, the nonbelievers, "represent not only the absence of values, but also the negation of values."[4] That is why they have to be either annihilated or isolated.

Musa A. Dube, a biblical scholar who teaches at the University of Botswana, argues that this religion from above legitimates a religion of conquest and exploitation. In her interpretation, the self-proclaimed "friends of God" imagine that all spaces on earth are available to them, and they use their religion as a passport that gives them access to every corner on earth.[5] Thus, Moses appears as a messenger elected by an unknown God, who is delivering a law given by a God whom no one has ever seen. This law is a license to subjugate all peoples of the earth in all places on earth. Dube contends that in the hands of Western powers, this type of religion was and remains a colonizing ideology to the detriment of Native Americans and indigenous people everywhere.

Arguing in a similar vein, Canaan S. Banana, who teaches religious studies at the University of Zimbabwe, proposes that Christians must rewrite the Bible "so that God can be liberated from dogmas that make God the property of ethnic syndicates."[6] She forcefully contends that the early Israelites identity as "God's chosen people became a justification for their conquering people in the land they viewed as a 'promised land'—promised to them by God as a reward for their faithfulness and as compensation for their suffering."[7] Later Christians used this concept of election to legitimate the subjugation of the tribes of Europe, to redeem the Holy Land from the infidel during the Crusades, and to exploit the native people of the "New World."

Bringing the argument closer to the United States, Canaan Banana quotes Josiah Strong, a clergyman and leader of the Social Gospel Movement in the United States at the end of the nineteenth century and in the early twentieth century, as saying, "far from lamenting the gradual disappearance of the American Indian...we should see in his extinction merely the reflection of the will of God in preparing the land for a better race."[8]

Josiah Strong spoke at a time when Social Darwinism and its theory of evolution, the survival of the fittest, racism, and a belief in progress blended with a political ideology of American exceptionalism and white supremacy. In Strong's theological universe, Native Americans represented a primitive level of social and spiritual development that was being superseded by a more advanced religion—Christianity. He explained the anticipated disappearance of Native peoples as the result of the inevitable moral and spiritual evolution of humankind. This evolution was the law of nature and the law of nature's God.

Warrior's challenge that we "put the Canaanite at the center" of our theology means that we have to abandon this theology of privilege and this notion of evolutionary progress, both of which are rooted in monotheism. In place of self-serving notions of privilege and progress, we need to fashion a nonusurpatious theology that does not justify the taking of the land of indigenous peoples or require Native Americans to adopt a foreign interpretation of the Exodus story as their story of hope. An interpretation of the Exodus narrative as a story of promise and fulfillment neither equips the church for dialogue with others in a multiracial and multicultural society nor adequately prepares us for the struggle for interracial justice.

In spite of the ways that the Exodus story has been used in the past to justify conquest, biblical scholar Walter Brueggemann cautions that "we completely misunderstand if we imagine that the laws of the Pentateuch are simply rules of order. They are, rather, acts of passionate protest and vision whereby Israel explores in detail how the gifts and vision of the Exodus can be practiced in Israel on an ongoing basis as the foundation for society."[9] Rather than interpreting revealed religion as a "passport" for conquest, he insists that we appreciate this "theology of coherence and rationality" for what it is.[10] Accordingly, the world and creation itself are not endlessly pliable. No one should create a private order to suit selfish personal wishes that trump the created order. God's sovereignty sets limits on human conduct, and these limits make human life and society possible. Brueggemann argues that events in Egypt, the gift of manna in the wilderness, and the decisive revelations at Sinai followed by conquest of Canaan reveal a transcendent reality that is beyond the "high claims and control of Egyptian pharaohs and Canaanite kings."[11]

While asking us to appreciate the strengths of this theology of moral coherence, Brueggemann cautions us to interpret it with a hermeneutic of suspicion, for it is open to exploitation and abuse. He knows that theological claims of rationality and order are subject to political claims of sovereignty and totalitarianism. Top-down theology can become top-down politics.

This then is our problem: How do we come to a theology of moral coherence, rationality, and order, while also avoiding political claims of sovereignty and totalitarianism? To address this pressing situation, we must reimagine our understanding of the character of God and show how a revised understanding of God can lead to a nonusurpatious social order.

Reimagining the Character of God

Brueggemann suggests that there are polar images of God in the Bible and that these two images must be kept in tension with each other. To embrace one and ignore the other results in a distorted and dysfunctional theology. He labels one aspect of God "aniconic" (meaning imageless) and the other iconic.[12] The latter can be understood as legitimating social structures, the former as the transformative tradition that embraces the pain caused by these same structures. The tension between these two is "definitional for Israel's understanding of God, for Israel's characterization of human persons, and for Israel's strategy for organizing public life."[13]

God's aniconic nature is free, unencumbered, and unpredictable. This enigmatic God is able to create fresh historical possibilities where none exist and to exercise sovereignty that Brueggemann says will "

brook no rival, entertain no alliance and share no splendor." Brueggemann asserts in this same passage: "Yahweh's imageless character
means that Yahweh is disengaged from the ways of worldly power." He
adds that it is precisely this "imageless identity of Yahweh that makes
Yahweh available for and attentive to those who do not participate in
the image-making, image-enhancing, image-producing, and image-
consuming ways of imperial life."[14] God's aniconic presence precludes
partnership with any earthly empire.

It is Yahweh's unencumbered nature that allows Yahweh to hear
the cries of the oppressed and to challenge and oppose all claims of
empire. Brueggemann's contention is that only an aniconic deity can
be allied with people who are marginalized and excluded from the
safe and privileged places of the world. So interpreted, the sociological
counterpart of Yahweh's aniconic character is an aniconic community—
one that refuses to assign form and structure to political community
in ways that will validate a disproportionate sharing of goods and
power. As Brueggemann states, "An *imageless* God accompanies *a social
vision* and *social practice of equality and justice*."[15] It is precisely Yahweh's
radical freedom—the freedom of an unseen God—that allows Yahweh
to engage in the social experiment of creating a radically egalitarian
community.

The laws and codes of the Torah are intended to embed the will
of this aniconic God in social practices and political policies. These
practices are most clearly enshrined in the laws of the sabbath year and
the jubilee year but also are seen in various laws mandating hospitality
to the stranger and treating others with kindness. The aniconic God
births an aniconic community that is radically egalitarian and racially
hospitable. Three hallmarks of this community are: (1) ending economic
exploitation and political subjugation, (2) establishing the normative
practice of radical hospitality within and across boundaries, and (3)
overturning traditional markers of differentiation. In other words, deep
solidarity is a manifestation of the presence of the aniconic God.

Brueggemann cautions, however, that "Yahweh's radical freedom
put Yahweh's faithfulness to Israel at risk."[16] Israelites in the wilderness,
like all people, had a need to locate God, and this means to create a
representation of or location for God—the golden calf or a temple.
Humans require some tangible expression of God's presence and
power. In the wilderness, the Hebrew people resort to making a golden
calf. Once settled in the Promised Land, they build the Temple. The
underlying interest these and other iconic representations serve is our
need for security and order, which are spiritual needs as much as they
are political motivations.

The deep and very human longing for security and order creates
a connection between iconic religious practices, social policies of

stratification, and the consolidation of political and economic power in some classes with the attending marginalization of other classes. In essence, our experience in the wilderness—our insecurity—drives us to trade radical freedom for assurances of security, order, and the validation of our way of life. Making such a trade is our human way of taming (civilizing) the wilderness.

Interpreting the Pentateuch through the lens of the iconic-aniconic paradigm moves us away from the promise-fulfillment paradigm of biblical interpretation and leads us toward a biblical interpretation that connects our need for social order with an understanding of the imperative to fight against the injustices created by the same. Whereas an iconic interpretation legitimates social structures that meet our need for security, order, and the legitimation of our way of life, an aniconic interpretation identifies primarily with experiences of pain caused by those same structures. As a result, rather than accepting binary structures of civilized/uncivilized, Christian/heathen, white/red, we are able to adopt a more dynamic and dialogical model. Instead of holding on to a metaphysical paradigm of promise-making and promise-keeping, we can adopt a bipolar theology of structure and struggle.

Whereas in the Jewish tradition this struggle between order and reformation is located in a polar theology rooted in an aniconic and iconic deity, in Christianity this struggle is defined by Christ—who is both human and divine, crucified and risen. Christ, the incarnate one, embodies divinity and humanity as coequals. Christ the crucified one embodies deep solidarity with the marginalized and the outcast. Christ the risen one manifests the new egalitarian order.

Understanding Christ, the crucified and risen one, in this way creates what Joerg Rieger calls "Christological surplus."[17] This Christ shows us a kind of love that resists paternalism, refuses to be assimilated by empire, and responds to the presence of the Other with deep solidarity.

In this iconic-aniconic framework, order and opposition replace promise and fulfillment as our primary theological paradigm. Brueggemann proposes that a theology of struggle is a "primary paradigm that is emerging among scholars."[18] This paradigm shift away from promise-fulfillment theology toward a theology of structure-struggle matters enormously to the mainline church in a postapology era because it allows the church to distance itself from an officially optimistic theology with its attending socio-political creed of evolutionary progress and assimilation, and to adopt a dialogical model that embraces socio-political reformation that is consistent with the liberation of marginalized and oppressed people, and the reformation and liberation of people held captive by the status quo.

I contend that the mainline church is more likely to envision itself as an agent of social transformation that is prepared and willing to challenge the legitimacy of prevailing social structures—structures that it helped create and from which it benefits—if it organizes its social vision around a polar theology of structure and struggle rather than relying on an organizing principle of promise and fulfillment and its binary vision.

This proposed change in orientation is a radical departure from the traditional Exodus mythology of deliverance and conquest. But it is a necessary change because it opens space to create a new basic narrative that is more in line with Robert Warrior's challenge that we begin to read the Bible with Canaanite eyes. We need to keep both poles in tension with each other. An iconic faith alone tends to assume blessing and order and seeks to assimilate, isolate, or annihilate people who do not share in the blessings and whose existence poses a threat to the continued enjoyment of the blessings. An aniconic faith alone tends to devolve into an atomistic faith composed of existential moments of protest and angst. We need both images of God in tension with each other so that we can engage in the difficult but hopeful work of social reconstruction.

NOTES

[1] Laurel C. Schneider, "Monotheism Defined," *Beyond Monotheism: A Theology of Multiplicity* (London: Routledge, 2008), 20.

[2] Ibid., 20.

[3] Ibid., 23. Her reference is David Hume, *The Natural History of Religion* (Stanford, CA: Stanford University Press Iamblichus, 1956), 23.

[4] Frantz Fanon, *The Wretched of the Earth*, translated by Constance Farrington (New York: Grove Press, 1968), 41.

[5] Musa W. Dube, "Savior of the World but Not of This World: A Postcolonial Reading of Spatial Construction in John," R. S. Sugirtharajah, *The Postcolonial Bible*, 118–35.

[6] Canaan S. Banana, "The Case for a New Bible," R. S. Sugirtharajah, ed., *Voices from the Margin: Interpreting the Bible in the Third World* (Maryknoll, NY: Orbis Books, 1997), 69–82, 69. This chapter is a reprint from *Rewriting the Bible: The Real Issue*, I. Mukonyou and F. J. Verstraelen (eds.). (Gweru: Mambo Press, 1993), 17–32.

[7] Ibid., 73.

[8] Ibid., 74. For the quotation from Josiah Strong, Canaan cites Thomas F. Gossett, *Race: The History of an Idea in America* (New York: Schocken Books, 1965), 178.

[9] Walter Brueggemann, "Bodied Faith and the Bodied Politic," *Old Testament Theology: Essays on Structure, Theme and Text*, ed. Patrick D. Miller, (Minneapolis: Fortress Press, 1992), 78.

[10] Brueggemann, "A Shape for Old Testament Theology I: Structure Legitimation," ed. Miller, *Old Testament Theology*, 1–21, 16.

[11] Ibid., 7.

[12] Brueggemann, "Old Testament Theology as a Particular Conversation: Adjudication of Israel's Sociotheological Alternatives," *Old Testament Theology*, 118–49.

[13] Ibid., 118.

[14]Ibid., 122.

[15]Ibid., italics original, 125. In footnote 19, Brueggemann credits M. Douglas Meeks, *God the Economist: The Doctrine of God and Political Economy* (Minneapolis: Fortress Press, 1989) for this "pivotal insight."

[16]Ibid., 129.

[17]Joerg Rieger, "Christological Surplus," *Christ & Empire: From Paul to Postcolonial Times* (Minneapolis: Fortress Press, 2007), 315–16.

[18]Brueggemann, "Old Testament Theology as a Particular Conversation," *Old Testament Theology*, 138.

PART FOUR

Reconstruction

Reconstruction, the third dimension in Yamamoto's model of interracial justice, means "reaching out in constructive ways to heal." Reconstructive action requires "efforts to remake and retell stories about the self, the other, and the relationship."[1] Reconstruction focuses on creating a new future, not on explaining the past. But the church cannot change the future without being transformed itself. New wine must be poured into new wineskins (Mt. 9:17). The old mission to "civilize and Christianize Indians" is no more. The new social order is not yet. To be an agent for the construction of a new social order, the church must reform itself.

The reformation of the church is not a smooth, uniform process. We cannot assume that the denominational apologies proffered mean that every member of the denomination agrees with the apologies or that every member is prepared to enact their promises. They are not. Still, the denominations that have issued apologies acted at their respective national meetings, duly called. The voting delegates at these assemblies acted on behalf of the whole church. Because the vote was a collective action, it is not necessary that all the individual members of a denomination agree with every aspect of the apology. The apology does not require or assume unanimity in the church. But because it was an action taken by a duly authorized representative body, the apology does set a direction for the future.

NOTE

[16]Eric K. Yamamoto, *Interracial Justice: Conflict & Reconciliation in Post-Civil Rights America* (New York: New York University Press, 1999), 191.

8

The Journey of Repentance

The U.S. government offered its apology to Native Americans in 2009; it was buried in Public Law 111-118, Section 113 of the Defense Appropriations Act of 2010 (H.R. 3326). Noteworthy as it was, the apology has been criticized for the manner in which it was done and for its lack of specificity. President Obama signed the apology in a private ceremony shielded from the press. It was not read in public until May 2010. Importantly, the apology specifically identified a number of wrongs, recognized the history of Native American genocide and broken treaties, and expressed deep regret. However, the federal apology did not admit any liability for harm done. There was no transfer of land, no willingness to limit the plenary power of Congress over Native land, and no monetary compensation for damages. Finally, the apology pointedly eschewed support for any existing or future claims against the government that indigenous peoples might file. It was a thin apology.

In contrast, the apology issued by the Canadian government to First Nations peoples in 2006 was a thick or dense apology. The Canadian government paid $2 billion to aboriginal peoples who were forced to attend residential schools (the Canadian term for boarding schools). In 2008, Canada's Prime Minister Stephen Harper publically apologized to former students of the residential schools, and the government established a Truth and Reconciliation Commission.[1] The relationship between the Canadian government and First Nations peoples is still contested at many points. There are unresolved issues, and the government has been accused of prolonging the reconciliation process unnecessarily. That said, the difference between the policies of the two governments is glaring.

The Mainline Church in Transition

Since the United Church of Christ issued its apology to Native Americans in 2003, other denominations and individual congregations have issued apologies for their participation in Indian boarding schools and for their involvement—directly and indirectly—in the history of

Native genocide. The General Convention of the Episcopal Church in America issued an apology on July 17, 2009.[2] Collegiate Church, the first Protestant Church in New York City, issued its apology to Native Americans on November 29, 2009. In 2010, United Presbyterian (USA) congregations in Lancaster, Pennsylvania, were joined by local leaders of the Quaker and Mennonite denominations in issuing an apology to Native Americans "for the acts of the Paxton militia that massacred 20 peaceful Indians in Lancaster in 1763."[3] In 2011, on the 147th anniversary of the Sand Creek Massacre, "in a spirit of repentance," the General Commission on Christian Unity and Interreligious Concerns of the United Methodist Church apologized to the Cheyenne and Arapaho peoples for this atrocity and donated $50,000 to the National Park Service to support a learning center at the site of the massacre. The following year, the United Methodist General Conference approved a formal "Act of Repentance to Indigenous Persons" and committed itself to begin a process of healing of relationships between indigenous communities and the church. The Church Council of the Evangelical Lutheran Church in America apologized to Native Americans and Native Alaskans on December 12, 2012. This sampling of history shows a growing consensus among denominations in the mainline church that apologies are warranted and that the denominations are prepared to take steps to create new relationships.

In addition to offering separate apologies, mainline denominations acting in concert through the National Council of Churches have called for a celebration of Indigenous People's Day instead of Columbus Day. They also have joined with Native Americans in calling for an end to the public use of negative stereotypes and logos that are demeaning to Native peoples. These are substantive, life-affirming efforts to construct a healthier relationship between the mainline church and indigenous peoples and to change the public perception and attitude. Demystifying the past by correcting the legend of Christopher Columbus and changing the disingenuous and degrading characterization of Native Americans in our society are ways of anticipating a future in which racial stereotyping will no longer be tolerated.

In addition, a growing number of mainline denominations have repudiated the Doctrine of Discovery—an archaic doctrine that was formulated in the European Age of Discovery and Conquest when, with the blessing of the church, kings claimed a divine right to rule the earth. In June of 2009, during the 76th General Convention of the Episcopal Church, the Episcopal House of Bishops unanimously approved a resolution entitled "Repudiate the Doctrine of Discovery."[4] Presiding Bishop Katharine Schori spoke of the church's action as a "matter of healing." She said:

I urge you to learn more about the Doctrine of Discovery and the search for healing in our native communities.

But this is also a matter for healing in communities and persons of European immigrant descent. Colonists, settlers, and homesteaders benefited enormously from the availability of "free" land, and their descendants continue to benefit to this day. That land was taken by force or subterfuge from peoples who had dwelt on it from time immemorial—it was their "promised land." The nations from which the settlers came, and the new nations which resulted in the Americas, sought to impose another culture and way of life on the peoples they encountered. Attempting to remake the land and peoples they found "in their own image" was a profound act of idolatry.

Repentance and amendment of life are the answer, and God asks us all—this Church, our partners and neighbors, and the nations which were founded under the Doctrine of Discovery—to the challenging work of reconciliation.

The abundant life we know in Jesus Christ is made possible through sacrifice—through repairing what is broken, and finding holiness and healing in the midst of that challenging work. That work is often costly, but it is the only road to abundant life.[5]

The Philadelphia Religious Society of Friends repudiated the Doctrine of Discovery in December of 2009. The Unitarian Universalist Association of Congregations followed suit at their annual meeting in January of 2010, and the United Church of Christ did so at its denominational gathering in 2013.

Repudiating the Doctrine of Discovery is not an insignificant action. It puts the church in opposition to the Marshall Trilogy and the plenary power of Congress. It also may call into question the existence of Native American reservations. If there is no right of discovery and no attending right of conquest, in what sense can the government maintain the claim that it is reserving the land for use by Natives?

Ward Churchill helpfully reminds us that in addition to repudiating the Doctrine of Discovery, which is rooted in the divine right of kings, the fight to restore Native sovereignty questions some aspects of English common law.[6] Under English common law, the right to own land depends on the demonstrated willingness of the owners to develop their land in accord with the scriptural obligation to exercise "dominion" over it. Thus, entitlement to own land depends on the ability of a person to convert the "wilderness" to a domestic or "civil" purpose. The fact that Native Americans had developed well-established agricultural practices and land management programs long before the English arrived was simply not recognized by the settlers, even though they often depended for their survival on crops the Native Americans grew and on their hospitality.

The Powhatan Indians, the Natives of New England, and other Native Americans did not have English-style harbors because their watercraft did not need them. They did not practice deforestation or enclosure as the English did because their spirituality taught them to live in harmony with the land, not exercise dominion over the land. The common law tradition was as foreign to the Natives as the Christian theology that the missionaries preached.

One of the critical issues that will determine whether or not the mainline church becomes an ally of Native peoples in challenging the English common law tradition is the interpretation of Genesis 1:26, which reads: "Then God said, 'Let us make man in our image, after our likeness, and let them have dominion over the fish of the sea, over the birds of the air, and over the cattle, and over the all the earth, and over every creeping thing that creeps upon the earth.'"

Today Christians are divided in their interpretation of the meaning of "dominion." Some Christians interpret "dominion" to mean "exploitation" of the land and its resources. In this view, the earth and its resources are commodities. Other Christians interpret "dominion" to mean "stewardship." Rather than exploiting the earth as a commodity, stewardship means practicing sustainable, environmentally friendly ways. If the mainline church comes to a firm consensus that the latter meaning holds, then it seems possible and perhaps even likely that the church will find common cause with Native Americans on a number of pressing issues related to the environment and our stewardship of the land. Further investigation of this possibility is beyond the scope of this book, but the possibility, if seized, may become common ground for Christians and Native Americans who practice their traditional ways.

Since 1990, the World Council of Churches and the National Council of Churches and member communions have supported the "Justice, Peace and Integrity of Creation" (JPIC) initiative. They have adopted programs calling for a "Just, Participatory and Sustainable Society." When the JPIC priority was officially endorsed by the United Church of Christ, Norman Jackson, a ministerial colleague in the United Church of Christ and a member of the Seneca Nation, told me that it was the right priority but the wrong order. He said that from an indigenous person's perspective, the integrity of creation comes first, not last. I hope that the church is evolving toward a consensus agreement with his insight.

Adopting a stewardship theology would, in my opinion, make it more likely that the church would take a stand against what Ward Churchill calls "internal colonialism."[7] As he explains, internal colonialism is an oxymoron because by definition colonialism requires that a body of water separate the colonizer from the colonized. Thus, it is correct to say that England established colonies in North America, but it is not correct to say that the United States established colonies within its own territorial boundaries because there is no body of water separating the so-called lower forty-eight states from each other. However, Churchill contends that "internal colonization is the result of a peculiarly virulent form of socioeconomic penetration wherein the colonizing country literally exports a sufficient proportion of its population to supplant (rather than enslave) the indigenous population of the colony."[8] In the United States the Anglo-European settlers broke free from England and subsequently colonized indigenous populations. Framing the Native drive for self-governance in this context allows Churchill and others to argue that the struggle of indigenous peoples is not an expression of human freedom, but a fight to end foreign occupation of their land.

Now is the time to begin reaching out to heal the wounds from the past inflicted by internal colonialism. Yamamoto suggests that the South African Truth and Reconciliation Commission can serve as a model for the people and institutions prepared to commit to work for interracial justice in the United States.[9] While there is no direct parallel between the situations, one can imagine that there are parallels between the Bantustans—the all-black enclaves or homelands with limited self-government—in apartheid South Africa and the system of Native American reservations in the United States. When Nelson Mandela, the leader of the African National Congress, was elected president of South Africa after the fall of apartheid, one of his first presidential acts was to sign the Promotion of National Unity and Reconciliation bill, which established the Truth and Reconciliation Commission. The purpose of the commission was to bring healing to a wounded nation. The church could endorse a similar plan here.

The Truth and Reconciliation Commission in South Africa had three tasks: (1) investigate gross violations of human rights, (2) consider amnesty for those who confessed to political crimes, and (3) recommend reparations for victims. The social and political goals were to establish principles of accountability and the rule of law, generate respect for human rights, develop a human rights culture, and provide some measure of justice. The paramount task was to promote interracial healing and reconciliation. This is a task that the postapology church has also identified for itself.

The United Church of Canada gives us an even closer example of the work of a Truth and Reconciliation Commission, which I discuss below. Native Americans have created boarding school committees to investigate the policies and practices of these schools, recommend reparations for victims, establish principles of accountability, generate respect for human rights, and promote healing. The church could and should initiate similar programs as part of its commitment to promote healing and pursue interracial justice. Yamamoto underscores this imperative: "If those with power intend to retain their power over others and their attending privileges, then no apology will lead to reconciliation—the kind of release that transforms the relationship and liberates it from the legacies of the distant and recent past."[10] The kind of reconciliation Yamamoto speaks of in this passage is found on the other side of theological, institutional, and social transformation.

The United Church of Canada and First Nations Peoples

A brief introduction to the history of the apology of the United Church of Canada is in order, since most people in the U.S. mainline church are unfamiliar with it.

In the nineteenth and early twentieth centuries, approximately 150,000 children were removed from First Nations, Métis, and Inuit families and placed in residential schools. Some of these schools were private institutions affiliated with the schools of Henry Pratt or modeled after his philosophy. Other residential schools were run by the church. The programs and intent of the residential schools in Canada were similar to those of the Indian boarding schools in the United States.

According to the United Church of Canada website,[11] the church issued two apologizes to First Nations peoples. The moderator (the church's elected leader) apologized in 1986 "for the times in which the church had linked acceptance of European culture and the corresponding suppression of First Nations cultures to the sharing of the gospel of Jesus Christ." This apology did not make direct reference to residential schools, but the schools were an important part of the national policy of suppression/assimilation. This apology was acknowledged but not accepted by the church's General Council in 1988.

Later, in 1994, the United Church of Canada established a Healing Fund "to address the impacts of residential schools on Aboriginal peoples." Then, in 1997, the General Assembly, the national governing body of the church, approved "The Statement of Reconciliation" and committed the church to "a journey of repentance."[12] This statement was the church's formal apology for its complicity in the residential school system. The statement reads in part:

> The apology arose out of a sense of a corporate sin of commission for those times in which we had participated in the system. It was also tied to the sin of omission for those times in which we had not spoken out corporately against the national policies and practices which gave rise to the school system.

The church marked the twentieth anniversary of the 1986 apology on May 2, 2006, by signing a Residential School Settlement Agreement and pledging to contribute $6,891,170 to a Compensation and Healing Fund. The church acknowledged that this was a substantial financial commitment but not a fulfillment of its moral obligation.[13] Significantly, the church has fully funded its pledge.

Commendable as the church's conduct has been since its apology, it has not been without controversy. Eagle Strong Voice (Kevin Annett), a former pastor in the United Church of Canada, has been a leading critic of the apology. Initially he accused the church of making "pseudo-apologies." To substantiate his allegation, he produced a film, *Unrepentant: Kevin Annett and the Canadian Genocide*, released in 2007. On March 16, 2008, he and forty-nine others entered the sanctuary of Rosary Catholic Church in Vancouver, British Columbia, during morning worship. They walked to the front of the sanctuary and, in reference to the number of children who died while attending residential schools, unfurled a banner that read, "All the children need a proper burial."[14] The church responded to these charges with its own investigation, but it has not been able to substantiate Strong Voice's claim regarding the number of children who died while attending residential schools.

In an effort to empower indigenous peoples, Strong Voice called for the church to restructure itself and become more of a federation of cultures rather than a centralized bureaucracy with a national office. However, instead of embarking on such a radical change, in conversation with aboriginal peoples the United Church of Canada more modestly created the All Native Circle Conference in 1988 and partially funded it. Through this ethnically-defined conference, First Nations peoples who are members of the United Church of Canada have a degree of self-governance, and they have a voice in all matters of church governance. Members of the All Native Circle Conference voted not to disaffiliate from the denomination or to advocate for the dissolution of the church.

Some mainline denominations in United States have taken actions not unlike the action of the United Church of Canada when it created the All Native Circle Conference. But generally speaking, the governing bodies in mainline denominations are defined geographically, not ethnically or racially. A district, region, conference, or diocese—denominations have different titles—is usually a geographically defined entity. The bishop, regional minister, or conference minister is the administrative and spiritual overseer of churches in each area. Historically, denominations have resisted efforts by racial and ethnic groups to create their own governing bodies defined by race or ethnicity rather than by geography. However, strict adherence to geographic boundaries is breaking down. Some denominations are experimenting with racial and ethnic governing bodies akin to the All Native Circle Conference, but this is not a general practice.

In addition to creating the All Native Circle Conference, the United Church of Canada established a Truth and Reconciliation Commission to hear the stories of former residential school students and to help it chart a path for the future. In a presentation to that Commission in 2007, James V. Scott, the church's General Council Officer for Residential Schools, identified six characteristics of an apology that is genuine and substantial.[15] First, an apology must be an acknowledgment of responsibility. This validates the experience of those who have been victimized by violence and begins a process that can lead toward the offender's own healing by shattering the façade of innocence. Second, an apology must demonstrate some understanding of the harm that has been caused. Third, an apology must be accompanied by demonstrable acts of contrition, with a proviso that future acts will follow as more history comes into the light of day. Fourth, an apology must show a willingness to make reparation, which in this case includes listening to the stories of indigenous people that have been ignored for so long, settling claims arising from past wrongs, supporting efforts to recover languages and traditions that have been either lost or suppressed, and challenging both attitudinal and institutional racism. Fifth, an apology must be accompanied by a demonstrated commitment to build future relationships based on the principles of equality and respect. Sixth, an apology must ask for forgiveness, understanding that only those who have been aggrieved have the power to forgive.

The "Journey of Repentance," the official title of the process adopted by the United Church of Canada, includes several concrete steps to bring healing to the relationship between the United Church of Canada and First Nations people. It will be a demanding and hope-filled journey for the church. Canada is already an officially multicultural nation with two recognized national languages. Indigenous and ethnic communities are allowed and encouraged to maintain their traditions and identities. While anti-indigenous sentiment is still strong in some parts of Canada, and indigenous peoples express frustration with the slow pace of change, the reconciliation process cannot and will not be abandoned. The "Journey of Repentance" adopted by the United Church of Canada can be a constructive resource for the mainline church in the United States. We do not need to wait any longer to take additional steps on our own journey of repentance.

NOTES

[1]Mary Annette Pember, "The Quiet American Apology to Indians," *The Daily Yoder*, December 13, 2011. http://www.dailyyoder.com/quiet-american-apology-indians/2011/12/13/3634. Accessed 3/14/2015.

[2]Audrey Whitefield, "Episcopalians Apologize for Treatment of Native Americans," World Faith News, Nov. 9, 1997. Source: Anglican Communications News Service, Nov. 7, 1997, Canon John Rosenthal, Director of Communications Office, London. www.archive. wfn.org/1997/11/msg00092.html. Accessed 9/2/2014.

[3]Melissa Nann Burke, "Presbyterian churches plan apology to American Indians." *York Daily Record. York Sunday News*, 10/7/2010. www.ydr.com/ci_16259924?source=most_emailed. Accessed 9/7/2014.

[4]General Convention of the Episcopal Church 2009 Archives Research Report, Resolution 2009-DO35, "Repudiate the Doctrine of Discovery." The following website documents a number of significant actions taken by the General Convention of the Episcopal Church.
http://www.episcopalarchives.org/GC2009/09_nic/2009-D035.pdf. Accessed 12/14/2015.

[5]Katharine Schori, "Repudiation of the Doctrine of Discovery." The Domestic and Foreign Mission Society. The Episcopal Church. Copyright 2015. www.episcopalchurch. org/page/doctrine-discovery-resources. Accessed September 2, 2014.

[6]Ward Churchill, *Struggle for the Land: Indigenous Resistance to Genocide, Ecocide and Expropriation in Contemporary North America* (Monroe, ME: Common Courage Press, 1993), 37.

[7]Ibid., 23–26.

[8]Ibid., 23.

[9]Yamamoto, *Interracial Justice*, 254–75.

[10]Ibid., 271.

[11]"Right Relations: United Church Apologies to First Nations Peoples," http://www.united-church.ca/aboriginal/relationships/apologies.

[12]United Church of Canada, "Remembering the Children," http://www.rememberingthechildren.ca/press/ucc-apology.htm. See also, The World Council of Churches Central Committee, "The United Church of Canada: Working in Solidarity Toward Reconciliation," 26 August—3 September, 2002. https://www.oikoumene. org/en/resources/documents/central-committee/2002/the-united-church-of-canada-working-in-solidarity-toward-reconciliation

[13]"Background Documentation: The Indian Residential Boarding Schools Settlement Agreement," http://www.united-churchca/aboriginal/schools/statements/060502. The Anglican, Presbyterian, and United Church of Canada apologies are on the website http://www.united-churchca/aboriginal/schools/trc. Accessed 12/14/2015.

[14]Documentation and personal testimonies can be found at http://hiddenfromhistory. org/ and http://hiddenfromhistory.org/VoicesoftheCanadianHolocaust/tabid. Links to apologies by the Anglican Church, the Presbyterian Church, and the United Church of Canada and other useful information on the history and recent developments may be found at http://www.united-church.ca/aboriginal/schools. It is estimated that 150 First Nations, Métis, and Inuit children attended the residential schools. Strong Voice contends that fifty thousand children died, but this number is contested.

[15]http://www. United Church of Canada Press Release, "General Council to Reflect on Truth and Reconciliation," August 6, 2009.

PART FIVE

Reparation

Reparation means "to repair." Reparative justice requires the transfer of hard assets—land and money—and political power to indigenous communities. Yamamoto says that reparation means "enabling those harmed to live with, but not in, history."[1] He stipulates that reparation be grounded in group, rather than individual, rights and responsibilities. This requirement does not detract from the importance of individual responsibilities and initiatives, which I believe are essential, but it does mean that the actions of individuals are not sufficient. Therefore, we must begin working for reparative interracial justice with changes in the fiscal policies and the land policies of the church.

Reparation does not displace charity and kindness, but it demands more than changes in personal deeds and attitudes. Acts of charity and kindness, however well-intended, can be misinterpreted or have unforeseen or unintended consequences. There are many hidden dangers that might undermine or discredit charitable actions. For example, monetary gifts, mission trips to reservations, and outreach programs intended to promote healing can assuage feelings of white guilt without attendant attitudinal transformation and institutional restructuring and thus ultimately perpetuate oppression. Prolonged litigation of contested Native American claims can deepen grievances and solidify antagonisms. Competing interests can cause parties to misconstrue the intentions and actions of others and perpetuate paternalism and victimization. The potential problems are many. Because of the presence of these and other real and potential difficulties, the quest for interracial justice must focus on demonstrable results. Good words and good will are not enough.

The church must work for reparative justice for the sake of its credibility as a witness to the gospel. Working for reparative justice will be one of the defining features of Christian discipleship in the twenty-first century. In the realm of reparative justice changing the way white liberal Christians manage the hard assets of money and of land on both personal and institutional levels are two pivotal issues.

It is not enough to protest against the impoverishment of Native American reservations or grieve the ongoing exploitation and appropriation of native lands. Beyond protest we have to create new policies and practices that are viable alternatives to the present system. For only when we know that there is another way do we have the freedom to make informed choices.

NOTE

[1]Eric K. Yamamoto, *Interracial Justice: Conflict & Reconciliation in Post-Civil Rights America* (New York: New York University Press, 1999), 203.

9

An Economy in the Service of Life

When the mainline church apologized to Native Americans, it was not only expressing deep regret for the past but also voicing a profound hope for a new and radically different future. But this future is not inevitable. If we want to chart a new course leading to a different society in the future, we must address the structural conditions that create the present situation of economic inequality, oppression, and exploitation of Native Americans, and we must expose and overturn the value assumptions that validate these conditions.

We cannot create a new future in which interracial justice is normative by relying on an economic model that validated and continues to validate cultural genocide. The stark choice is between an economy that marginalizes Native Americans—and increasingly displaces members of the middle class—and an economy in the service of life. This is the context in which the struggle for interracial justice is taking place. Neutrality is not an option, because neutrality amounts to an endorsement of the status quo—and a betrayal of the apology. Christian discipleship in the postapology period will involve what Dietrich Bonhoeffer famously called "costly grace."

Sacred Land and the Resolution Copper Mine

The struggle between the San Carlos Apache Nation and the Rio Tinto Company puts a human face on this struggle. The Resolution Copper Mine is a project of the Rio Tinto Company, a multinational Australian corporation, and its partner BHP Billiton, an Anglo-Australian company. Development of the proposed mine has been delayed for almost a decade because of lawsuits filed by the San Carlos Apache Nation. But on December 12, 2014, Congress cleared the way for these two global mining companies to swap land with the government and proceed with the project. The legislation that authorized the land swap was included as an amendment to the National Defense Appropriations bill. This action by Congress effectively bypassed the Apache Nation's efforts to protect their sacred land by thwarting the development of the Resolution Copper Mine.

103

The land swap gives the companies developing the Resolution Copper Mine access to 2,400 acres of federally owned land in the Oak Flat area of the Tonto National Forest in exchange for 5,300 acres of the company's pristine private land, and it allows the two foreign companies to build a $6 billion copper mine on the site. The Resolution Copper Mine will be the largest copper mine in North America and one of the largest copper mines in the world. According to the company's website, once the mine is operational, it will supply the United States with more than a quarter of the nation's demand for copper for several decades, create more than 3,700 jobs, and pay more than $220.6 million in annual wages.[1] Unquestionably, the Resolution Copper Mine will have a positive impact on the regional and national economy. It will create jobs, provide incomes, generate taxes, and supply the country with an essential resource—copper.

However, the copper deposit is buried 7,000 feet below the earth's surface. The technique used to extract the copper is called "block cave mining." The method involves removing tons of underground rock. Removing the rock creates underground tunnels or caverns and the potential for cave-ins. In addition, the toxic waste produced by the mine is likely to be deposited on the earth's surface. The Resolution Copper Mine will completely destroy the Oak Flat topography.

The San Carlos Apache Nation opposes the Resolution Copper Mine and the land swap because the Oak Flat area is sacred territory for its members. The federal government acknowledged this in 1955. When it agreed to the land swap, the government unilaterally and abruptly withdrew this recognition and the protection that went with it. Sacred land that the San Carlos Apaches believed was protected for future generations became a commodity by congressional fiat.

James Anaya, a Regents' Professor at the University of Arizona Rogers College of Law who served on the United Nations Human Rights Counsel from 2008–2014, describes the congressional authorization of the land swap as a victory for Rio Tinto, a foreign-owned mining company, and "a shameful circumventing of democratic process in the face of environmental concerns and potential violations of the religious and cultural rights of the Apache people."[2]

Defenders of the land swap point out that Congress has the legal authority to make the swap, and as a result of the swap, the government will gain control of more land. They also give assurances that environmental concerns will be addressed in extensive studies that are yet to be done. Rio Tinto executives are on record as promising that the company will follow the guidelines established by the International Council on Mining and Metals and United Nations standards. These standards require the free, prior, and informed consent of indigenous peoples and full respect of their rights. However, congressional authorization of the land swap was not predicated on the San Carlos Apaches' consent, and the company is not legally obligated to abide by UN standards.

The Resolution Copper Mine raises a number of difficult questions for the mainline church in the postapology era. If the federal government can designate and undesignate at will what is and what is not a sacred site, we have to question the value of federal designations of any and all sacred sites. Does the church's repudiation of the Doctrine of Discovery have implications for this situation? Does economic expediency trump the rights of people? In a nation in which we will all soon be minorities, we must be concerned about the rights of all minorities. In a multicultural society, do some religious communities have more rights than others? Are some sacred sites more sacred than others? Economist Robert Heilbroner chillingly notes that "a society ruled by the market will be an attentive servant of the rich, but a deaf bystander to the poor."[3]

What is to be done?

Reinhold Niebuhr chided: "The sum total of the liberal Church's effort to apply the law of love to politics without qualification is really a curious medley of hopes and regrets."[4] He acknowledged: "Liberal Christianity has not been totally oblivious to the necessary mechanisms and techniques of social justice in economic and political life. But the total weight of its testimonies has been on the side of sentimental moralism." Niebuhr bluntly warned: "The Christian who lives in and benefits from, a society in which coercive economic and political relationships are taken for granted, all of which are contrary to the love absolutism of the gospel, cannot arbitrarily introduce the uncompromising ethic of the gospel into one particular issue."[5] Moral certitude is not a convincing argument.

Niebuhr not only questioned the efficacy of perfectionist absolutes but also urged liberal Christians to acknowledge that "In modern society the basic mechanisms of justice are becoming more and more economic rather than political, in the sense that economic power is the most basic power. Political power is derived from it to such a degree that a just political order is not possible without the reconstruction of the economic order. Specifically this means the reconstruction of the property system."[6]

Behind the Veil of Economics[7]

What is this economic power to which Niebuhr refers in the above paragraph? What is the source of the raw power that brushed aside the rights of the San Carlos Apache Nation and allowed Congress and the developers of the Resolution Copper Mine to desecrate the sacred ground of this tribe? Joseph A. Schumpeter explains in *Capitalism, Socialism and Democracy*:

Bourgeois society has been cast in a purely economic mold: its foundations, beams and beacons are all made of economic material. The building faces toward the economic side of life. Prizes and penalties are measured in pecuniary terms. Going up and going down means making and losing money....In part it appeals to, and in part it creates, a schema of motives that is unsurpassed in simplicity and force. The promises of wealth and the threats of destitution that it holds out, it redeems with ruthless promptitude.[8]

Expanding on this insight, Schumpeter notes that, "The fundamental impulse that sets and keeps the capitalist engine in motion comes from the new consumer goods, new methods of production or transportation, the new markets, the new forms of industrial organization that capitalist enterprise creates." He identifies this "impulse" as the "process of Creative Destruction," which he also calls "the gale of Creative Destruction." This dynamic of Creative Destruction, Schumpeter says, is "the essential fact of capitalism."[9]

Karl Polanyi taught us that capitalism is embedded in social institutions.[10] It can exist only in a society that allows for and rewards what Schumpeter describes as the process of Creative Destruction. The political, social, and cultural institutions of society—what Schumpeter calls the "beams and beacons"—are molded and shaped by the economic foundation on which they rest. In a market society, economic institutions are at the base, not the apex, of that society.

The need for new markets and new products, cited above, points toward the often cited law of supply and demand. According to a commonplace and carefully constructed narrative, the economy in a market society is governed by the law of supply and demand and regulated by price mechanisms and competition. The creation of goods and services and their distribution is not predetermined by a centralized planning agency or dictated by an external value system. The marketplace is "value neutral." This means that what happens in the marketplace is determined by the give-and-take of autonomous rational individuals acting in their own self-interest in competition with other individuals who are similarly motivated. Competition and price mechanisms regulate both the creation and the distribution of goods and services.

Thus, a spokesperson for the Resolution Copper Mine could reasonably argue that if there were not a demand for copper and if the technology needed to dig the mine did not exist and if there were no way to bring the copper to market, there would be no mine. Demand creates the need. Technology supplies the means to meet the need. The market holds out the promise of wealth for those who take advantage of the opportunity presented and the threat of destitution for those who are not prepared to seize the moment. In the rarified atmosphere of market neutrality, the decision to open the mine is simply a matter of supply and demand. This is how the free market operates.

Charles L. Schultz, who served as the Chairman of the Council of Economic Advisors in the administration of Lyndon Johnson, offers a strong defense of the free market in *The Public Use of Private Interest*. While he allows that there is a place for government oversight and regulation of the economy, which he calls "normative economics," Schultz asserts that the competitive marketplace is best at "harnessing the 'base' motive of material self-interest to promote the common good." Indeed, he contends that "harnessing the 'base' motive of material self-interest to promote the common good is perhaps *the* most important social invention mankind has yet achieved." Underscoring this point he adds, "turning silk into a silk purse is not a great trick, but turning a sow's ear into a silk purse does indeed partake of the miraculous."[11]

Schultz's defense of capitalism is not a straw argument. Robert Heilbroner writes in *21ˢᵗ Century Capitalism* that "capitalism has altered the course of history first and foremost by creating an entirely new socioeconomic environment in which, for the first time, material conditions have improved steadily and markedly in those areas where the system flourished." Looking back over a period of 150 years, stretching from the 1830s to the 1980s, he concludes that per capita income in the United States grew enough "to double real standards of living every forty-seven years."[12] That is no small accomplishment. It is, in fact, remarkable.

With some rudimentary aspects of capitalism set before us, we can entertain two basic criticism of it. The first criticism focuses on assumptions about self-interest and the nature of competition. The second criticism focuses on a more overtly political argument.

Amartya Sen, a Nobel-prize-winning economist, offered a sharp critique of doctrine of self-interest in a series of lectures he delivered in 1986. The lectures later became the basis for his book *On Ethics and Economics*. In these lectures, Sen argued that political economists who rely on the doctrine of self-interest as the engine of the marketplace would do well to paraphrase Dante and adopt as their motto "Abandon all friendliness, you who enter!"[13] In a related lecture, he asserted that the notion of self-interest as it is commonly used in conventional economic theory is not only "*ethical* nonsense" but "*deceptive* nonsense," and those who rely on it are guilty of "anti-ethicalism."[14] Driving his point home, he said that "universal selfishness as *actuality* may well be false, but universal selfishness as a requirement of *rationality* is patently absurd."[15] The notion of universal selfishness is anti-ethical because it discounts, and more strongly disallows, consideration of any other values such a loyalty, friendship, concern for others, or environmental sustainability.

If we want to create a people-oriented society, a society in which friendliness and other values are taken into account, we need an economic model that makes ethical sense, not one that relies on ethical nonsense.

The more overtly political argument against unfettered capitalism comes from two political science professors, Jacob Hacker and Paul Pierson. The title to their award winning book, *Winner-Take-All Politics: How Washington Made the Rich Richer—and Turned Its Back on the Middle Class*, states the case plainly.[16] Muddling through and awaiting change is not a viable strategy for at least two reasons. First, wealth is likely to become ever more concentrated in the hands of the more privileged members of society. Second, members of the middle class are likely to become disenchanted with the promise that the free market is "value neutral." We need a different system.

Economics in the Service of Life

It is often said that the past is not prologue. No one believes that the standard of living for people in the United States will double every forty-seven years in the next one hundred and fifty years, as it did between 1830 and 1980. At the same time, we cannot shake ourselves free of this memory. That is why Jung Mo Sung, a liberation theologian, writes in *Desire, Market and Religion*: "The pursuit of wealth has become the most important objective for the lives of the majority of people, particularly those integrated in the market. Commodities have become *the* object of desire."[17] People seek commodities and wealth not simply for the sake of wealth, or to gain status and power, or to satisfy insatiable desires, but because this is what it means to be an "American." Accumulation is a form of cultural validation.

In his classic political science study *The Liberal Tradition in America*, Louis Hartz argues that colonial Americans were "born free" and "born equal." In Hartz's theory of U.S. history, the first European settlers did not have to overthrow an entrenched feudal aristocracy, as did their counterparts in Europe. "Amid the 'free air' of American life," Hartz tells us, "something new appeared: men began to be held together, not by the knowledge that they were different parts of a corporate whole, but by the knowledge that they were similar participants in a uniform way of life—by that 'pleasant uniformity of decent competence.'"[18] They were guided by what Hartz describes as an "irrational attachment" to the political philosophy of John Locke who, Hartz contends, "dominates American political thought, as no thinker anywhere dominates the political thought of a nation."[19]

This "pleasant uniformity of decent competence" feeds into a belief that the United States is a meritocracy—a classless, open society in which upward mobility is possible. This belief Hartz identifies as "the master assumption of American political thought," an assumption rooted in "the reality of atomistic social freedom."[20] The idea of social liberty and social equality is, Hartz says, "the distinctive element in American civilization."[21]

Because white Americans have a creedal belief that we are all born free and equal, we do not frame political issues in terms of class struggle but as the tension between majority rule and minority rights. This way of framing issues is favorable to conventional market theory and the touchstone doctrine of self-interest because an expanding economy benefits the majority and creates opportunities for social mobility. Theoretically everyone, even people on the margins of society, will benefit from an expanding economy. Fairness simply means that opportunities for personal betterment are created, and some "reasonable" degree of protection is afforded for the rights of the minority.

Hartz's analysis helps us understand why the notion of class is almost anathema to white liberals who cherish the notion of a free and open society, and why white liberals are so often unable to move from recognition and responsibility (the first two dimensions of interracial justice) to reconstruction and reparation (the last two dimensions of interracial justice). To admit that ours is a class-ruled culture violates our belief that this is an open society in which free and equal people are upwardly mobile and our confidence in the neutrality of the market. Yet Yamamoto reminds us that reconstruction "entails active steps (performance) toward healing the social and psychological wounds resulting from disabling constraints."[22] The dynamic of reconstruction runs counter to the meaning of atomistic individualism and our belief in an open society.

So, what is to be done?

We have to begin with a candid assessment of our situation, disabuse ourselves of the idea that ours is a free and open society, and come to terms with the reality of social and economic class. Only then can we develop an alternative economic model that connects ethics and economics.

Religion and Class

G. William Domhoff, a research professor at the University of California, Santa Cruz, has been studying and writing about power and class in the United States since 1950. He finds that because of our attachment to the ideal of social mobility, most Americans resist talking about power and prefer instead to talk about influence. However,

Domhoff reports, class and power are very real, and social mobility is "very rare and often a matter of luck."[23]

Instead of an open society, Domhoff contends that what we actually have is a class-based and governed society that is built on four interlocking or overlapping power networks: economic, political, military, and religious. Each network can be turned into a strong organizational base for wielding power. The networks can work independently of each other, or they can be aligned with each other to form a powerful coalition. The individual networks are not necessarily in competition with each other. There is no ingrained system of checks and balances.

In addition to identifying power networks, Domhoff identifies three different indicators of power: (1) Who benefits? (2) Who governs? (3) Who wins?[24] He contends that people who occupy important institutional positions and who take part in important decision-making groups have power. They are the ones who have the ability to initiate, modify, or veto policies; the ones who govern; and the winners in a winner-take-all economy.

People who have power form alliances and social networks that determine who will become part of their network and who will be excluded. While their ability to make this determination is not absolute, membership in certain social organizations, educational pedigree, and wealth function as parts of a gate-keeping system that monitors who is in and who is out. The fact that upward mobility—entrance into this network—is rare suggests that the members of this network—the upper class—have established generational continuity. Because membership in the upper class is partly based on ownership of profit-producing investments, it is a capitalist class as well as a social class. Members of this class are concerned with "such matters as the investment climate and the rate of profit. That is, they have a capitalist mentality."[25]

As the reality of class becomes more apparent, the notion of an open society in which upward mobility is possible becomes more ephemeral. Therefore, an increasing number of middle-class Christians will likely experience a growing dissonance between the marketplace concepts of "self-interest," "market neutrality," and "upward mobility," and their own self-interest. The disparity between capitalist mentality and the core gospel value of the "royal law," according to which "You shall love your neighbor as yourself" (Jas. 2:8) will become so stark that it will demand accountability and action. This commandment, which is at the heart of liberal Christianity, will demand that we create an economic model that makes sense, instead of continuing to rely on an economic model that is nonsense and anti-ethical. We need economic tools—concepts and measures—that will help us translate the mandate to love our neighbor into economic policy.

Connecting Ethics and Economics

We do not need to abandon the marketplace, declare ourselves enemies of capitalism, or juxtapose spiritual concerns with material needs. But we do need to change the way we measure economic value and reward behavior. And we need to do it now.

In *Justice in an Unjust World*, Karen Lebacqz tells us that if we want to seek justice, we "must begin with the realities of injustice....Injustice is our lived reality, and...it is therefore the primary category."[26] The quest for justice must be grounded in experience, not theory. For Christians this quest often begins with the question: Who is my neighbor? Jesus answered this inquiry with the Parable of the Good Samaritan (Lk. 10: 29–37). While members of the mainline church and others tend to interpret this parable in highly individualistic terms as encouraging acts of charity, I think that a better interpretation is to understand we have a responsibility to stand in deep solidarity with those who have suffered injustice. The parable calls us to see that the pursuit of justice is a mutual enterprise that involves not only the Samaritan, but also the inn keeper and perhaps many others. The economic resources of both the Samaritan and the inn keeper are put at the disposal of the one who is in need. The Samaritan's promise, "Take care of him; and whatever more you spend, I will repay you when I come back" (Lk. 10:35), is both unconditional and unlimited. That should tell us something about the meaning of deep solidarity.

We saw earlier that Reinhold Niebuhr chided liberal Christians for our tendency to absolutize the law of love and ignore the realities of coercive economic and political power. He put his finger on some painful truths. We have for the most part failed to translate individual ethics to institutional practices and policies. As a result, we often experience a disconcerting disconnect between the moral values we profess and the economic policies and practices we embrace. The cause of this problem is in part the fact that we have lacked the proper tools to connect ethics and economics. The conventional economic model that puts selfishness at the center of rational decision-making does not allow for an ethic of other-regard. Likewise, our cultural bias toward a heightened sense of individual autonomy militates against an ethic of deep solidarity. But society is more than the aggregate sum of its individual members. We need to recover the idea that the purpose of the economy is the well-being of all of the members of society.

Economists Joseph Stiglitz, Amartya Sen, and Jean-Paul Fitoussi address the concept of well-being in *Mis-Measuring Our Lives: Why the GDP Doesn't Add Up*. The Gross Domestic Product (GDP) and the Gross National Product (GNP) are standard ways to measure and track economic performance. These are aggregate figures that measure production levels. GDP and GNP data give economists and policy-makers important information that allows them to gauge the level of economic output in various sectors, and to make policy adjustments. Increasingly, GDP and GNP data are being interpreted as measures of societal well-being. It is this use of the data that gives rise to the authors' concerns and to their claim that we are "mis-measuring our lives." In order to correct this situation, they propose that we *"shift emphasis from measuring economic production to measuring people's well-being*...put in the context of sustainability."[27]

Stiglitz, Sen, and Fitoussi make a number of recommendations for evaluating well-being: (1) *look at income and consumption rather than production*, (2) *emphasize the household perspective*, (3) *consider income and consumption jointly with wealth*, (4) *give more prominence to the distribution of income, consumption and wealth*, (5) *broaden income measures to non-market activities*.[28] The authors also identify eight dimensions of well-being: (1) material living standards, (2) health, (3) education, (4) personal activities, (5) political voice in governance, (6) social connections and relationships, (7) environment, and (8) insecurity.

The metric of well-being allows for the measurement of income, consumption, and wealth at a household and individual level. It also provides data for longitudinal studies to indicate whether a particular situation is improving or deteriorating. Finally, well-being allows for comparative analysis within, between, and among communities. So, well-being is a very comprehensive metric.

Through the lens of well-being, social inequalities and their underlying causes become readily apparent. Solutions may not be easy to find or create, but situations will be understood in a comprehensive way so that measures can be taken to address the disparities in ways that are consistent with the goal of creating a people-oriented society, which should be our long-term goal.

The tradition of the sabbath year and the jubilee year can help us connect our ethics and our economic policies and priorities. These ancient laws were instituted to be a safeguard against a return to the economics of oppression and exploitation and appropriation. The purpose of these laws and more broadly of this tradition was to preserve community.

The loss of community is a result of what economist Franz Hinkelammert calls an "antiutopian theology" that "replaces palpable reality—the real material life of human beings—with a reality made up of mental constructs, in whose name it condemns palpable reality."[29] In this same passage, Hinkelammert reminds us that sharing goods is foundational to the Christian message. Sharing is necessary because it is a theological imperative. When community is denied, God is denied.

Hinkelammert illustrates his point with reference to the story of Ananias and Sapphira. This infamous couple is arguably sentenced to death. Hinkelammert argues, "Refusing to share goods with the community is pride. It is the only sin for which the foundational Christian message recognizes the death penalty (Acts 5:1-12). This is community of goods in the fullest sense, having everything in common" (233). He adds, "God punishes him [Ananias] with death." Hinkelammert contends that their "sin" is not hoarding; it is spiritualizing community. Instead of following the example of Ananias and Sapphira and fabricating a spiritual community that denies the real thing, we must be mindful of the second great commandment to "love your neighbor as you love yourself" (Mk. 12:31). It is in the flesh and blood reality of community that we encounter the aniconic God who challenges the institutional structures of oppression. This is the God who, as Karl Barth said, "takes His stand unconditionally and passionately...against the lofty and on behalf of the lowly, against those who already enjoy right and privilege and on behalf of those who are denied it and deprived of it."[30] If we do not get involved in the struggle to safe-guard the well-being of every community, we might miss the reality of God altogether.

The primary concern of a church committed to interracial justice is not charity—helping those in need—although this is important. The primary concern is to end oppression, exploitation, and expropriation and to promote the flourishing of healthy communities because this is where we encounter God. The mainline church's relationship with Native Americans is an opportunity for the church to find its way back to this gospel message and to the God who is revealed in Jesus Christ— the incarnate, crucified, and resurrected one who is always present in places of struggle.

The mainline church's apology to Native Americans was a courageous step in this direction. As we continue on this path, the global church can be an important partner for the mainline church. The World Council of Churches (WCC) has been engaged in pioneering work in the field of economic reform. The mainline church has been slow to actively embrace the wisdom of the WCC, but I continue to hope that this situation will change as the social demographics and economic reality of the church continue to change.

In 1987, Ulrich Duchrow, regional secretary for Mission and Ecumenical Relations with the Evangelical Church in Baden, Germany, wrote *Global Economy: A Confessional Issue for the Churches?*[31] A series of important international consultations followed the publication of this book, and several study documents have been published as a result. Through this process of study and discussion, the WCC has taken the position that the global economy is a "confessional issue." By taking this stance the WCC is saying that the global economy, and specifically the ideology of the free market, is an idolatry that challenges the very heart of the gospel and the integrity of the faith.

In 2000, the WCC released "Alternative Globalization Addressing People and Earth (AGAPE)," a study document for use in congregations. This was followed by "A Call for Love and Action" in 2006. In 2014, The Greed Line Study Group of the WCC issued its report.[32] Authors of this report found that "unbridled greed" is a primary source of global economic growth. They argued that in order to fight poverty we must fight greed and the excessive concentration of wealth, because the wealth of the have-gots is directly related to the poverty of the have-nots. The Greed Line Study Group concluded that three of the most detrimental effects of greed are poverty, income and wealth inequality, and environmental degradation.

Since the 1980s, the WCC's analysis of the global economy has evolved. In the United States the response to the work of the WCC has been stronger and more positive in academic circles than in denominational circles. Yet I have hope. Members of the mainline Protestant church are also evolving in their understanding of key economic issues and in their willingness to take a public stand on those issues. As this evolution continues, global Christianity can become an important source of encouragement and a resource for the church in the United States.

Ulrich Duchrow acknowledges that one of the important lessons learned by members of the church who have engaged in a serious study of the economy is that "it is the poor who evangelize us and not we who evangelize the poor."[33] This awareness turns the traditional model of mission inside out. The mainline church is the body that needs to be evangelized and converted to the gospel through its encounter with the world, and especially through deep solidarity with people who are marginalized by the have-gots. From a Christological perspective, we must develop a theology of encounter. Through sustained encounter with Christians in the global church, most of whom are poor, persecuted, and not white, and through sustained encounter with Native American communities, the church can be evangelized and transformed into a more potent force for interracial justice. The rule of concreteness—standing in deep solidarity with the made-poor and the marginalized members of society—will lead the church into new and demanding territory. It may also renew the church and put a right spirit within us.

The rule of concreteness brings us face to face with the practice of radical discipleship, which is modeled in the Gospels and throughout the New Testament. The admonitions to feed the hungry, cloth the naked, and heal the sick are not calls for charity; they are strategies for making disciples—for creating and sustaining communities of discipleship that are prepared to challenge the status quo and work to transform it. Such a community of faith embodies what Ulrich Duchrow calls the "contours of discipleship." He says: "The contours of a discipleship group begin to emerge whenever family, possessions and self-determination are set at risk for the sake of the kingdom of God and God's justice and the way of discipleship is accepted."[34] He draws an outline of discipleship from experiences of the liberation church in Latin America, which he believes could be adapted by the more affluent churches in the Northern Hemisphere.

At the time that he was writing *Global Economy* in the 1980s, Duchrow hoped that the church in Europe and the church in the United States would model themselves after base communities that were so important in the reformation of the church in Latin America in the early days of liberation theology. That has not happened. But the marginalization of the middle class and the expanded use of well-being as a measure of the economy may yet give rise to a new social movement in the church. Perhaps the Occupy Movement (which broke out on the streets of New York in 2011 and quickly spread across the nation), Black Lives Matter, and La Raza presage this possibility.[35]

The contours of discipleship begin to take form when Christians create intentional communities and willingly place themselves at risk for the sake of the gospel. This is the first defining line of discipleship. The Journey of Repentance developed by the United Church of Canada is one example of a denominational body moving in this direction. The public repudiation of the Doctrine of Discovery is another example of a church body taking some risk for the sake of discipleship.

Duchrow suggests that the second contour of discipleship comes into focus through education. The mainline church needs to take a bolder and more direct approach to discipleship training and adult education. Native American scholars, some of whom I have referenced in this book, are teaching us things we did not learn in school about our own history. They are providing important correctives to the misshapen history that glorifies the United States as a white Christian nation built upon European and Greco-Roman values. Postcolonial biblical scholars and liberation theologians are opening up basic texts to new understandings. Indeed, the confessing church, the church in struggle, must become part of our daily experience.

A third contour of discipleship that Duchrow identifies is a willingness to cooperate with secular groups. For models, the church might look at the Truth and Reconciliation Commission of South Africa or the Truth and Reconciliation Commission in Canada. The church can also learn from the healing practices in its own tradition and the healing practices of Native Americans. Both Christian traditions and Native American traditions have well-established practices of nonviolence and truth-telling that are transformative. The pathways and opportunities for cooperation are here; they do not need to be invented, only taken.

Lastly, Duchrow encourages church organizations and institutions to look to the universal church for wisdom and council. The experiences of the WCC in fostering a process for dialogue on the global economy can be helpful. Today the majority of Christians in the world are not white or affluent and do not live in the United States or Europe. They are people of color, often poor, and members of minority communities. The old order, which was celebrated in the 1893 World Exposition in Chicago, is gone. We need to wake up.

NOTES

[1]"The Resolution Copper Project," resolutioncopper.com/the-project/. Accessed 1/4/2015.

[2]James Anaya, "Rio Tinto should make some lands off limits to mining and abandon the project if it can't gain local support," *The Arizona Republic*, December 28, 2014. http://www.azcentral.com/story/opinion/op-ed/2014/12/29/resolution-copper-mine-con/20865771/. Accessed 1/4/2015. Malia Zimmerman, "Fed land swap gives go-ahead to Arizona's 1.6 B-ton copper mega-mine," FoxNews.com, December 23, 2018. http://www.foxnews.com/politics/2014/12/23/fed-land-swap-gives-go-ahead-to-arizona-16b-ton-copper-mega-mine/. Accessed 1/4/2015.

[3]Robert Heilbroner, *21st Century Capitalism* (New York: W. W. Norton & Company, 1993), 108.

[4]Reinhold Niebuhr, *An Interpretation of Christian Ethics* (Cleveland: The World Publishing Company, 1963), 160.

[5]Ibid., 163, 167 respectively.

[6]Ibid., 165.

[7]This heading is taken from Robert L. Heilbroner, *Behind the Veil of Economics: Essays in the Worldly Philosophy* (New York: W. W. Norton & Company, 1988). The veil of economics to which the title refers is the presumed neutrality of the law of supply and demand and related assumptions. Behind the veil of economics is an ideology: "a set of belief systems to which the ruling elements of the society themselves turn for self-clarification and explication," 47.

[8]Joseph A. Schumpeter, *Capitalism, Socialism and Democracy* (New York: Harper & Row, Publishers, Torchbooks, 1950), 73.

[9]Ibid., 83.

[10]Karl Polanyi, *The Great Transformation: The Political and Economic Origins of Our Time* (Boston: Beacon Press, 1957).

[11]George L. Schulz, *The Public Use of Private Interest* (Washington, D.C.: The Brookings Institution, 1977), 18.

[12]Heilbroner, *21st Century Capitalism*, 56.

[13]Amartya Sen, *On Ethics and Economics* (Oxford,: Blackwell Publishers, 1992), 1.

[14]Ibid., italics original, 31.

[15]Ibid., italics original, 16.

[16]Jacob S. Hacker and Paul Pierson, *Winner-Take-All Politics: How Washington Made the Rich Richer—and Turned Its Back on the Middle Class*, (New York: Simon & Schuster, 2010).

[17]Jung Mo Sung, *Desire, Market and Religion* (London: SCM Press, 2007), 1.

[18]Louis Hartz, *The Liberal Tradition in America: An Interpretation of American Political Thought Since the Revolution* (San Diego: Harcourt Brace Jovanovich, Publishers, 1955), 55.

[19]Ibid., 6, 140 respectively.

[20]Ibid., 62, passim.

[21]Ibid., 63.

[22]Eric K. Yamamoto, *Interracial Justice: Conflict & Reconciliation in Post-Civil Rights America* (New York: New York University Press, 1999), 175.

[23]G. William Domhoff, *Who Rules America? Power, Politics, and Social Change* (New York: The McGraw-Hill Companies, Inc., 2006), fifth edition, 63.

[24]Ibid., 13–17.

[25]Ibid., 75.

[26]Karen Lebacqz, *Justice in an Unjust World: Foundations for a Christian Approach to Justice* (Minneapolis: Augsburg Publishing House, 1987), 10.

[27]Joseph E. Stiglitz, Amartya Sen, Jean-Paul Fitoussi, *Mis-Measuring Our Lives: Why GDP Doesn't Add Up* (New York: The New Press, 2010), 10.

[28]Ibid., italics original, 11–14

[29]Franz Hinkelammert, *The Ideological Weapons of Death: A Theological Critique of Capitalism*, trans. from Spanish by Phillip Berryman (Maryknoll, NY: Orbis Books, 1986), 232.

[30]Joerg Rieger, *No Rising Tide: Theology, Economics, and the Future* (Minneapolis: Fortress Press, 2009), 130. Citation is Karl Barth, *Church Dogmatics*, vol.2:1, ed. G. W. Bromley, trans. George Eliot (New York: Harper Torchbooks, 1957), 386–87.

[31]Ulrich Duchrow, *Global Economy: A Confessional Issue for the Churches?* Trans. by David Lewis (Geneva: WCC Publications, 1987). Duchrow credits the Lutheran World Federation meeting in Dar-es-Salaam in 1977 as first identifying the economy as a confessional issue for the church because of its systematic exclusion and oppression of certain groups of people, 47.

[32]The Report of the Greed Line Study Group of the World Council of Churches. Members of the group included: Lucas Andrianos, Edward Dommen, Bob Goudzwaard, Rosario Guzman, Clement Kwayu, Carlos Larrea, Konrad Raiser, Jung Mo Sung, and Michael Taylor. Athena Peralta consolidated the report. https://www.oikoumene.org/en/resources/documents/wcc-programmes/public-witness-addressing-power-affirming-peace/poverty-wealth-and-ecology/the-report-of-the-greed-line-study-group-of-the-wcc. Accessed July 18, 2015.

[33]Duchrow, *Global Economy*, 193.

[34]Ibid., 64.

[35]Joerg Rieger and Kwok Pui-Lan explore this possibility in *Occupy Religion: Theology of the Multitude* (Lanham, UK: Rowman and Littlefield, 2012). The authors argue, "One of the most important insights of modern theology in that we can know God only in relation to us....Justice is practiced in the formation of relationship and the restoration of abusive relationships not only with God but also with human beings," 97.

10

A Theology of Land and Life

Native Americans consider ownership of the land to be *the* central issue of our time. Interracial justice is not possible without a drastic change in the plenary power of Congress and other fundamental changes in the law regarding ownership and use of the land. From a Native perspective, Vine Deloria Jr. notes "that a fundamental element of religion is an intimate relationship with the land on which religion is practiced should be a major premise of future theological concern."[1] He adds elsewhere: "Recognizing the sacredness of lands on which previous generations have lived and died is the foundation of all other sentiments."[2]

Daniel Wildcat, a Yuchi member of the Muscogee Nation and an environmental scholar, speaks of "indigenous metaphysics."[3] He describes this experiential-based metaphysics as recognizing "at the most fundamental level this interconnectedness and relatedness of human beings to the earth." This recognition, he says, "provides the first principle of our rich spirituality. A spirituality that is literally grounded in our experience of the natural world as full of creation's power; a spirituality that denies the dichotomies that most often define Western religions."[4]

Elizabeth-Cook Lynn insists: "We must begin with the return of land for two reasons: first, there is no more important value to colonized people than the land; and second, it is in the land that the native finds his morality and religion, his life and his survival."[5]

Ward Churchill says:

> The intent here is not, no matter how much it may be deserved in an abstract sense, to visit some sort of retribution, real or symbolic, upon the colonizing or former colonizing powers. It is to arrive at new sets of relationships between the peoples which effectively puts an end to the era of international domination. The need is to gradually replace the existing world order with one which is predicated on collaboration and cooperation between nations. The only way to ever really

accomplish this is to physically disassemble the gigantic state structures—structures which are literally predicated in systematic intergroup domination; they cannot exist in any sense without it—which are evolving in this imperialist era.[6]

Moving from a more general discussion of the importance of the land to a specific example, in the language of the Lakota the name for the Black Hills is *"Paha Sapa Wakan"* (Sacred Black Hills). The late Elden Lawrence, a Dakota and a member of the Sisseton Wahpeton Oyate (people) who served as President of Sisseton Wahpeton College in South Dakota for several years, tells us that for his Lakota relatives, "The Sacred Black Hills are central to their religion and culture."[7] And whereas "[t] he Native believes he belongs to the land,…the White man believes the land belongs to him."[8] He adds:

> Non-native people place themselves at the center of their own creation along with the pot of gold that is their real god. In a sense they create god in their own image. Conversely, traditional Natives have an almost instinctive awareness of a Supreme Being, and seldom do they question His existence. Rather, they question whether the Creator acknowledges their existence.[9]

U.S. law recognizes the sacred sites of native peoples. The American Indian Religious Freedom Act of 1978 (amended in 1994), the Religious Freedom Restoration Act of 1993, and The Native American Graves Protection and Restoration Act of 1990 are cited by Lawrence as illustrative of federal acknowledgement of the heritage of indigenous peoples and the importance of their relationship to the land. Yet material found on private property or on state land is exempted from these laws. In addition, the law places the burden of proof on those who want to protect artifacts. But tribes often lack the means, the technology, or the knowledge to protect their sacred sites and the human remains and other artifacts there.

Lawrence's reference to gold is particularly telling in the context of the history of the Sacred Black Hills. In the Lakota language *He* (a ridge of mountains) *Sapa* (black) is both a spiritual center and the homeland for the *Oceti Sakowin* people. The Lakota peoples are rooted in *He Sapa*. It is their place of origin. In the Lakota tradition, to be a human being means taking care of this sacred land that birthed them. The land is sacred to the Lakota because it is the land of their ancestors, and it is the source of their way of life. It is the sacred obligation of the Lakota to take care of the land, Mother Earth. Caring for *He Sapa* is one of the aspects of life that identifies a person as Lakota. To disrespect the land is to betray one's identity, one's place of origin, and one's ancestors.

For hundreds of years, Natives made pilgrimages to *He Sapa*. But in 1851 a Catholic priest, Father John de Smet, illegally ventured into Lakota territory.[10] De Smet later reported that he found gold in the Black Hills. In 1874, the federal government sent Lt. Colonel George Armstrong Custer and soldiers under his command on an expedition into the Black Hills to confirm Father de Smet's report. Though at first Custer's expedition found only small traces of gold, the news that there was gold spread quickly.

The 1868 Treaty of Fort Laramie established ownership of the Black Hills by the Lakota Nation. But the discovery of gold and the influx of white prospectors effectively vacated the treaty. In 1875 the government tried to negotiate a new treaty with the Lakota, but they refused. In response, the government transferred its relations with the Lakota from the Bureau of Indian Affairs to the Department of War. The Lakota were then informed that if they did not submit to the government's "request" to negotiate a new treaty, they would be considered "hostiles." What followed is known in standard history texts as "The Great Sioux War." From a Lakota perspective, this war was a series of unprovoked U.S. military invasions and treaty violations.

Thousands of miners flooded into Lakota territory during the Gold Rush of 1876, prompting Congress to draw new boundaries. Congress unilaterally declared: "Said Indians do hereby relinquish and cede to the United States all the territory lying outside the said reservation."[11] The town of Deadwood, South Dakota, sprang up overnight. The Homestake Mine was opened in Lead, South Dakota in 1878. It became the largest and deepest gold mine in North America and produced more than 40 million ounces of gold between 1878 and 2002, when the mine was closed.

The Lakota have consistently defended their right to the land as stipulated in the Treaty of 1851 and the Treaty of 1868. The dispute between the tribe and the government eventually came before the U.S. Supreme Court. On July 23, 1980, in *United States v. Sioux Nation Indians*, 448 U.S. 371 (1980), the Supreme Court recognized the right of Congress to exercise eminent domain over Native territory, but found that the Lakota had not been properly compensated for the land and the gold taken. The court ordered the government to pay Sioux Nation for the value of the land at the time it was taken plus interest and for the market value of the gold. The high court fixed the value of the award at nearly $106 million—a small sum when compared to the more than $18 billion taken by the Homestead Mine.[12] Leaders of the Sioux Nation refused to accept the settlement and demanded that the land be returned to them. They based their claim on the Treaty of 1868, which Congress ratified and which has never been revoked.

The government then noted that other tribes were involved and had to be consulted. The government's intent, it seems, was to create conflict between the Dakota and Nakota, who reside primarily in Minnesota and eastern North and South Dakota, and the Lakota, who reside mostly in western North Dakota and South Dakota.

So in May of 1994, the Lakota sponsored a Treaty Summit. Elden Lawrence, a Dakota, attended the Summit as a representative of the Sisseton and Wahpeton Sioux Tribe. He reports that when he got to the meeting his biggest question was: "What has this got to do with us?" The matter was between the Teton Lakota Nation and the United States. After a series of consultations with others, Lawrence reported that the people he represented supported the Teton Lakota, who have steadfastly refused to sell their treaty rights. Meanwhile, the interest-bearing account being held by the United States is valued in excess of $750 million and increasing.

A visit to the website of The Great Sioux Nation brings the dispute between the Lakota and the United States up to date and gives a deeper understanding of nationhood and Native sovereignty.[13] The website features a map of the land claimed by The Great Sioux Nation. The area includes the Standing Rock Reservation, the Cheyenne River Reservation, the Great Sioux Reservation, the Pine Ridge Reservation, the Rosebud Reservation, the domain of the Yankton Tribe and a large area identified as Unceded Indian Territory. The tribal claim to the Unceded Territory is based on the Treaty of 1851, which recognized Sioux Nation sovereignty over six to seven percent of the "lower 48" states.[14] Ensuing conflicts between whites and Native Americans led to a second Treaty of Fort Laramie in 1868. Article 2 of this treaty defined the boundaries recognized as Native American land and guaranteed that the area so identified was "set apart for the absolute use and occupation of the Indians herein named."[15]

The Unceded Territory claimed by the Sioux Nation forms a geographical area that covers a large part of what is now the state of South Dakota and extends south to Kansas and west to parts of Colorado. On the official U.S. government map, all of the reservations are separate and discreet isolated regions, and the Unceded Territory is not recognized.

The map allows us to imagine a future that is on the other side of internal colonization. It is a picture of what the Great Sioux Nation would look like if treaties were honored. The map also underscores the point that the Great Sioux Nation never ceded or sold any of its land to the federal government.

The involvement of Father De Smet and the ensuing history of the Black Hills War and the Gold Rush of 1874 give credence to Deloria's charge against the church: "Where the cross goes, there is never life more abundantly—only death, destruction and ultimately betrayal."[16] We who are Christians have to live with this history, but we do not need to be bound by it. We can create a different future. The church's renunciation of its mission to civilize and Christianize Native Americans and its repudiation of the Doctrine of Discovery encourage me to believe that the time is ripe for the church to turn away from the narrative of conquest and create a new identity narrative.

Creating a New Identity Narrative

The Bible is the basic text for Christians. Therefore, our search for a new identity narrative must begin with the Bible. But we must learn how to interpret it in a new key. The dominant methods of biblical interpretation in the liberal church have been heavily influenced by two motifs: an existentialist orientation or a "mighty deeds of God" theme. The former method of interpretation emphasized personal decision-making as an act of faith. The latter method of interpretation singled out decisive events around which Israel defined its faith. Both identified with categories of time and space (symbols of freedom) rather than with a sense of place—signifying commitment and belonging.

In *The Land*, Brueggemann suggests that the prioritizing of time and space has been a mistake. "It is now clear," he writes, "that a *sense of place* is a basic human hunger." In response to this hunger, he believes, we must recognize that "land is a central, if not *the central theme* of biblical theology."[17] Obviously, this change in orientation could have important implications for the future of theology in the liberal Protestant church and its relationship with Native Americans. But we need a theology of the land that is not usurpatious.

The existentialist orientation and the "mighty deeds of God" theme are being challenged, if not replaced, by a postcolonial interpretation of the Bible. In *A Postcolonial Commentary on the New Testament Writings*, Fernando F. Segovia says: "A central task of postcolonial reading...is to determine whether, within the context of colonialism, texts promote or contest the colonial order." He contends that power, hierarchy, and opposition are central concerns in postcolonial biblical studies.[18]

In "Discovering the Bible in a Non-biblical World," Kwok Pui-lan cautions that we must pay special attention to issues of power and truth-claims when we approach the Bible, for "truth is not merely something to be grasped cognitively, but to be practiced and acted out in the self-cultivation of moral beings."[19] She holds that in the future biblical interpretation must rely on "dialogical imagination," which is a process of "mutuality, active listening, and openness to what the other has to say." This process invites us to see other people, particularly people who do not share our faith tradition, not as objects to be civilized and

Christianized but rather as human beings to be welcomed as partners in a shared and ongoing search for truth.

In this postapology time, these more recent developments in biblical studies and theology provide a basis for looking for biblical traditions that resist colonization and nurture respectful dialogue across faith boundaries. As we look for such narratives, I appreciate a proposal proffered by Naim Ateek, a Palestinian Christian and founder of the Sabeel Ecumenical Liberation Theology Center in Jerusalem. He is writing in the context of Israeli-Palestinian relations, but the questions about contested ownership of the land with which he wrestles are germane to our situation in the United States.

Ateek believes that the Mosaic story of conquest is dysfunctional in the modern era in the Middle East and that in order to find peace, the people and governments of that region need to create a new story about the land. He urges governments and faith communities to reject the story of violent conquest of the Promised Land. He proposes that the Ezekiel tradition, forged in the time of Israel's return from Babylonian exile, is more responsible and fitting for the present.[20] As the Israelites prepared for life in their postexilic period, Ezekiel instructed them:

> So you shall divide this land among you according to the tribes of Israel. You shall allot it as an inheritance for yourselves and for the aliens who reside among you and who have begotten children among you. They shall be to you as native-born sons of Israel; with you they shall be allotted an inheritance among the tribes of Israel. In whatever tribe the alien resides, you shall assign him his inheritance, says the Lord God. (Ezek. 47:21–23).

The aliens are not to be annihilated or marginalized. Israel has to share the land with the people who live on it.

It is possible, of course, to read the Ezekiel passage as encouraging the assimilation of the aliens into Israel's culture. But now, given the church's renunciation of the mission to "civilize and Christianize Indians," this interpretation is hurtful, not helpful. Such a suggestion also misrepresents Israel's experience in exile. Brueggemann describes what this experience of exile meant for Israel: "Israel ended where it had begun, landless. The landless have no history. It takes land to make history. Israel had no land and therefore no history. It was over."[21] Displaced and dispossessed, the Israelites struggled to forge a new identity.

In a most radical way, God spoke through the prophet Ezekiel, who promised that Israel would return to the land, but this time a note of graciousness would replace the right of conquest.[22] This time Israel will receive the land as a gift, and aliens would be included.

When the exiles returned to Jerusalem, they confronted first the problem of syncretism and later Hellenization. Israel developed two seemingly opposite ways of dealing with the situation. We can think of these two ways as the Ezekiel tradition and the Ezra tradition.

As the cited passage from Ezekiel shows, in this tradition the Hebrew people were called upon to recognize the new demographic reality in the Promised Land. They were not free to create a society in their own image. They had to recognize that rights of indigenous peoples. Today, we might say that when the Israelites returned from Babylon, they experienced the Promised Land as a borderland—a place where differences needed to be respected and identities negotiated.[23] The postapology church is in a position to engage in borderland theology with Native Americans.

In contrast to the Ezekiel tradition, which called for negotiating with the indigenous peoples, the Ezra tradition, which is associated with rebuilding the Temple, is often interpreted in a more legalistic fashion. In this school of thought, Ezra represents the "hardliners." The Ezra tradition frowns on intermarriage and encourages cultic separatism. But Brueggemann suggests that the deeper issue addressed in the Ezra tradition is not cultic purity but rather how Israel would survive in history as a covenant people. He encourages us to think of the tradition associated with Ezra, Nehemiah, and the Levites not simply as a tradition of separatism but rather as an effort to order life, community, and the land in ways that are faithful to the covenant.[24] Thus, the Ezra tradition may be interpreted in the context of structure and struggle— the iconic and the aniconic God. Accordingly, the deep issue in the Ezra tradition is not purity for the sake of purity, but rather how Israel will faithfully embody the important political issues of human worth and economic dignity. As Brueggemann notes:

> Hellenization raised the issue about whether faith in Yahweh was possible and worth the price. The normative answer, given in Jerusalem and celebrated by the aristocracy who managed the bureaucracy and administered the temple, was that such faith had a low priority. Hellenization set a pattern for the knowing, uncaring rich to take advantage of the trusting, helpless poor.[25]

So understood, the tradition associated with Ezra has as much and perhaps even more to do with separating the faith tradition from corruption by the political elite as it does with separating the Israelites from the indigenous peoples. Thus, the Ezekiel tradition and the Ezra tradition are wrestling with two distinct and different problems. The Ezekiel tradition is dealing with the issue of multiculturalism as an external concern; the Ezra tradition is responding to the threat of corruption posed by the presence of an internal elite who might manipulate the tradition for their own benefit.

Likewise the church today must assess both the integrity of its witness in a multicultural world and its relationship with the uncaring elite who may be tempted to exploit the Christian tradition for their benefit.

I am suggesting that with its apology to Native Americans, the church is emerging from its own period of cultural captivity during which it either supported and encouraged the exploitation and subjugation of indigenous peoples or turned a deaf ear to their cries of protest. Now in this postapology, postexilic period, the church has an opportunity to redefine its relationship with Native Americans, with the land, and with the uncaring elite. This is where the renunciation of its former mission and the repudiation of the Doctrine of Discovery lead us. Now we have to face what Brueggemann describes as the "odd and discomforting.... biblical assertion that God wills land for his people and he will take it away from others for the sake of the poor."[26] We can begin a new dialogue between the mainline church and Native Americans about sacred sites and the land.

Sacred Sites

In "Sacred Places and Moral Responsibility," Deloria notes that Euro-Americans and Native Americans tend to have different understandings of what constitutes a sacred site.[27] For Euro-Americans, land becomes consecrated land because of human sacrifices made at a particular location. Battle sites and cemeteries are examples of consecrated land. These are sacred sites for white people. For Native Americans, locations are designated as holy or sacred because some higher power has manifested itself there. Since Natives do not usually interpret war as a sacred experience, as a general rule battlefields are not considered sacred sites, but other sites such as Oak Flats are sacred. Thinking about sacred sites in ways that are compatible with the ways of Native cultures would profoundly change the way we manage the land. Our theological paradigm could become biocentric or ecocentric as well as Christocentric.[28]

Protecting tribal sacred sites would have a huge environmental and political impact, particularly on those states that have the greatest number of these sites. In New Mexico, the Cochiti Pueblo needs 24,000 acres of land for access to and use of religious shrines in the Bandelier National Monument. They also have shrines in the Tetillia Peak Recreational Area, which is located within the boundaries of the Pueblo de Cochiti Indian Reservation. Members of the Santa Clara Pueblo are asking the Indian Claims Commission to set aside 30,000 acres that have religious and ceremonial importance for them, but these lands are in the control of the National Forest Service and the Atomic Energy Commission. In Arizona, the Hopi people have sacred shrines in the Black Mesa area, now leased to Peabody Coal. They have also identified sacred land in the Coconino National Forest. The Navajo Nation recognizes seven sacred mountains that are integral to their tradition, all in the public domain. These are only a few of the places that are sacred to Native peoples. Recognizing treaty claims and honoring the sacred sites of indigenous peoples is not simple. But it is necessary if we are to stop to the diminishment of aboriginal rights, which Cook-Lynn describes as "a movement of legalized genocide."[29]

Robert Williams argues that the recourse open to Native peoples is to directly confront and challenge both Congress and the U.S. Supreme Court. Appeals to international bodies like the United Nations and to documents like the United Nations Declaration on Indigenous Rights may be useful, but he believes that ultimately these matters will be resolved by the U.S. courts and by Congress. The church could and should stand with Native Americans and support their claims. The church could and should also help garner public support for Native American challenges to exploitive ways of managing the land. The Ezekiel and Ezra traditions can equip the church for this new mission.

Cautious Hope

I am cautiously hopeful that denominations that have issued apologies to Native Americans will create a new identity narrative that is consistent with the goal of creating a more just and peaceful society. Our intentions are in the right place. But unless we can align our passionate commitment for interracial justice with our economic values, we will stop at half-hearted measures. The experience of the mainline church in response to liberation theology is an illuminating and cautionary story.

In the 1960s, mainline denominations moved quickly to adopt the language of liberation theology coming from Latin America. But as Penny Lernoux documents in *Cry of the People: The Struggle for Human Rights in Latin America—The Catholic Church in Conflict with U.S. Policy*, the church's enthusiastic response to liberation theology did not translate readily into institutional practice.[30] People responsible for managing pension funds and for overseeing the economic investments of their respective denominations were disconnected from seminary classrooms and congregational pulpits where liberation theology was taught and preached.

Lernoux documents that eight mainline denominations were investors in Gulf Oil, which was prosecuted for paying bribes in Bolivia. The Episcopal and Presbyterian churches held stock in Kennecott Copper, one of the principal beneficiaries of the military coup in Chile.

The United Church of Christ purchased 1,000 shares in the Rockefeller-owned International Basic Economy Corporation and loaned the multi-billion dollar enterprise $250,000. Incredibly, the denominational leaders defended the loan as its Christian obligation to help developing nations. This sobering history should give us pause.

The decisions to invest in repressive regimes and exploitive corporations are not examples of "bad faith." They were decisions made by conscientious people who were guided by shared value assumptions and their legal obligations to manage funds prudently. Nonetheless, as Lernoux documents, criticism from some quarters within these denominations was sharp. She quotes a critic of the status quo, Robert McAfee Brown:

> [To acknowledge that] our entire social structure is sick at the core is not only a message we may not like, but a message with which we may not, in fact, be able to come to terms. It may challenge the social legitimacy of the kind of work we do to earn our incomes, it may leave us with nagging questions of why we are entitled to such splendid homes when most of the human family lives in substandard dwellings, and it may leave us unsure that the creation of a few splendid human relationships is really a sufficient answer to the not so splendid squalor that continues in the midst of those relationships.[31]

Lernoux concludes, "Commitment to change is not easy."

Still, liberation theology, with its central message of "the preferential option for the poor," has endured, and it continues to challenge the church. The mainline church's participation in the civil rights Movement and the voting rights movement and other campaigns to bring about systemic change are a reason to hope.

Let me cite one more case that makes me cautiously hopeful. On the centennial anniversary of the 1890 Battle at Wounded Knee, the then governor of South Dakota, George Mickelson, declared that 1990 would be a "Year of Reconciliation." To signify this event, the state legislature proclaimed that instead of celebrating Columbus Day, the state would henceforth recognize American Indian Day as part of its effort to reconcile with tribal peoples, who constitute about ten percent of the state's population. Since then, there have been additional efforts to improve relations between nonindigenous people and indigenous people in the state. The enactment in 2007 of the Indian Education Act by the state legislature, which mandates the development and use of a curriculum for understanding Native American history and culture, is an example of this effort. Since 1993, Professor Charles Woodard at South Dakota State University has facilitated an annual gathering of the Oak Lake Writers' Society to "contribute to the strengthening and preservation of Lakota, Dakota, and Nakota cultures through the development of culture-based writings."[32] It is also encouraging that a number of mainline denominations affirm and support Native American pastors, have educational program and centers in Native country, and host forums and conversations on racism. In some instances, mainline denominations are working with tribal members to establish clear title to land that the churches have held in trust for the tribes so that the land can be returned to the tribes. Finally, some mainline denominations have made very significant financial commitments to Native Americans as part of their quest for interracial justice.

We are in a time of "reverse mission." In the past white missionaries believed that they were bringing civilization and the gospel to Native Americans. Now Natives are teaching white Christians new ways to think about the gospel, the land, and the hallmarks of "civilization." As we learn to think about the land as a place to which we belong, rather than thinking of the land as something that belongs to us, those of us who are members of the white Anglo-Saxon Protestant tradition may also find new ways to think about our well-being, the well-being of others, and the well-being of future generations.

Finding an Alternative John Locke

For white people, learning to think about the land—property—in new ways is a monumental challenge. Ownership of private property is one of the sacrosanct foundations of Western society. To understand why, we must turn to the philosophy of John Locke. In the following I examine two radically different interpretations of Locke's theory of private property. One interpretation is based on the work of Louise Hartz. It is the more commonly held interpretation of Locke. The other is based on the work of Ulrich Duchrow and Franz Hinkelammert. This second interpretation is not as well known, but it is the one that we need to heed in our pursuit of interracial justice.

Hartz contends that "Locke dominates American political thought, as no thinker anywhere dominates the political thought of a nation."[33] He observes that the revolutionaries of 1776 and their English predecessors in America were not constrained by a feudal structure or a feudal ethos. They were "born equal."[34] And because they did not have to overthrow an established aristocracy and an entrenched bureaucracy, they were "born free." Hartz asserts: "Amid the 'free air' of American life, something new appeared: men began to be held together not by knowledge that they were different parts of a corporate whole, but by the knowledge that they were similar participants in a uniform way of life."[35] He concludes that these two natural conditions—born equal and born free—fed into "the master assumption of American political thought...the reality of atomistic social freedom."[36] Thus, individual equality and individual freedom, heralded as "self-evident truths," became the defining features of life for Euro-Americans.

Crucial to Hartz's interpretation of Locke is the idea that the institution of private property both necessitates the coercive power of government and limits the coercive power of government. Government must have the power and authority to protect private property and enforce private contracts, but at the same time the power of government is limited by the existence of private property and private contracts, both of which precede the formation of government. These assumptions, Hartz contends, shape the "American democratic personality."[37] So interpreted, Locke emerges as the defender of atomistic individual freedom, the champion of private property, and the spokesperson for limited government.

In sharp contrast to Hartz's interpretation of Locke's philosophy, Ulrich Duchrow and Franz Hinkelammert argue that Locke's theoretical feat was not the defense of atomistic individual freedom and limited government, but just the opposite.[38] They contend that Locke legitimated both the enslavement of indigenous peoples of North America and the taking of their land. In their interpretation, what Locke facilitated was "unprecedented genocide in the name of human rights."[39] Also, they assert that "guaranteeing property is just the same as declaring that the peoples of North America can be expropriated without condition or restriction."[40] To understand the reasoning behind this interpretation of Locke, we need to return briefly to the history of England.

As a result of the English Civil War fought in the 1640s and the Glorious Revolution of 1688, the English abolished the divine right of kings and established the right of habeas corpus (1679) and the English Bill of Rights (1689) These documents protected the rights of individuals against the unjust exercise of the coercive power of the state. However, at the same time that the English were establishing the rights of English citizens, they were capitalizing on the slave trade. John Locke himself invested in the slave trade and profited from it. So Locke and his contemporaries faced a dilemma: to defend human rights and to justify slavery simultaneously. This, according to Duchrow and Hinkelammert, was the problem that lay at the heart of Locke's political philosophy. And this is the reason that he bifurcated the state of nature and civil society.

For Duchrow and Hinkelammert, two items of particular interest flow from this bifurcation of nature and civil society. First, civil society is defined as the perfection of the state of nature. The state of nature is the antithesis of civil society, which rests on the foundation of private property and social contracts. Also, in Locke's theory money exists in the state of nature—before the creation of civil society. This assumption is not logical, but it was necessary for Locke to make this leap because it allowed him to develop a theory of alienation.

In the realm of nature there is a natural limit on the accumulation of goods. Things spoil, rust, or otherwise deteriorate over time in a state of nature. But money is fungible. There is no natural limit to the accumulation of money or its lifetime. Therefore, the abstract symbol (money) dominates the actual material commodity, which is subject to natural limits. A person can have only so many "things," but one can possess a limitless sum of money.

In Duchrow and Hinkelammert's interpretation, alienation is possible in the state of nature because the owner of property can sell it and thereby become alienated from it. Therefore, people who do not own property and people who sell their property and/or their labor are alienated from either their property or their labor or both. People so alienated may live in a civil society, but they are not and cannot be members of it. They have no voice in civic affairs. They have no rights because they are alienated from property, which is what makes a civil society both possible and necessary.

In Locke's theory people who are not members of civil society are enemies of it. By their very presence they are declaring war upon civilization. So members of civilization have a duty to defend themselves and all civilization against these "barbarians." There is, then, a perpetual state of warfare between "civilized" people and "uncivilized" people.

Not content to justify civilization's war upon the uncivilized, Locke was aware that he also needed to find a way to justify taking the land of the indigenous peoples. Kings could simply usurp the land of others by claiming that it was their divine right to do so, but civilized people could not act like kings. To solve this problem, Locke argued that barbarians must pay members of civil society for the expenses of war incurred by the peaceful defenders of humanity. Thus, the English invaders were not actually stealing the land of indigenous peoples. Rather, the uncivilized Natives were morally obligated to pay the civilized invaders for the cost of war waged upon them. Duchrow and Hinkelammert call this philosophy "an annihilation mentality."[41] They conclude:

> The European conquerors—so Locke sees it—come to North America with peaceful intentions. The peoples living there want, unlawfully, to thwart this. They put themselves in a state of war against these peace-loving conquerors. Here Locke even concludes that they want to make slaves of the conquerors. Consequently he concludes that these peaceful conquerors may treat the whole population like wild animals, and destroy them on the basis of the law of nature.[42]

In summary, Locke's theory proposes that civil society rests on the foundation of private property *and* social contracts. The presence of these two assumptions not only bifurcates the world of nature and civil society, it also means that civil society exists for and through a series of market relationships between and among property owners. As Canadian political scientist C. B. Macpherson argues in *The Political Theory of Possessive Individualism: Hobbes to Locke*, the cost of this cohesion "is a weakening of liberal institutions." People who do not own property and participate in the series of market relationships have no political voice. "It follows," Macpherson concludes, "that we cannot now expect a valid theory of obligation to a liberal democratic state in a possessive market society." We are left with "a new equality of insecurity among individuals."[43]

The pursuit of interracial justice entails a radical departure from the more conventional theory of private property, contracts, and civil society based on a traditional interpretation of the political theory of John Locke. Those of us in the mainline church require a new way to think about private property.

A Theology Fit for the Future

A biblical vision of creation begins with an affirmation that the earth is the Lord's. God is the Creator, and all of creation belongs to God. The sabbatical year and the jubilee year were instituted to remind the ancient Israelites and us of this reality. Ownership of the land is vested in God and is therefore subject to use according to the rules that honor God. There is no "empty land." There is no "right of discovery," There is no right of dominion, or right of conquest. We live on the land and belong to the land, but the land does not belong to us. The land belongs to God, and we are responsible for managing the land in ways that are respectful, sustainable, and support well-being. A responsible theology fit for the future begins with this affirmation.

While the idea that we do not have dominion over the land may seem novel to people schooled in John Locke's theory of ownership, it is a concept that is well grounded in the Christian tradition. Charles Avila, a Filipino activist who at one time served as the vice-president of the Federation of Free Farmers in the Philippines, has researched the understanding of property held by early church scholars and intellectual leaders who wrestled with the tension between their theologically informed theory of property and *dominium*, the understanding of property embodied in Roman law. In *Ownership: Early Christian Teaching*,[44] Avila examines a tradition largely forgotten by contemporary Christians, but one we should reclaim. For the most part, the following summary of the teachings of the Church Fathers is taken from Avila's study. The translations from original texts are his unless otherwise noted. Notes on Roman Empire and the definition of *dominium* are from Durchrow and Hinkelammert.

"The Roman Empire introduced a basic distinction between *possessio* and property (*dominium* or *proprietas*)."[45] *Possessio* means actually having a thing. *Dominium*, in contrast, refers to a more comprehensive form of ownership with the following features:

- *Dominium* is a full right that grants protection against withdrawal, against damage, against other effects; the owner enjoys complete freedom of use, including sale or destruction, and the right of inheritance. "*The core of this statement is the absoluteness of property and hence its designation as* dominium."[46]
- *Dominium* is related to the rule of paterfamilias (the power of the house-father over the family).
- *Dominium* contains no relational elements. There are owners and there are nonowners in society. In some instances, the law may prohibit intermarriage between the owner class and nonowners.
- Partial rights, such as pledge rights or securities, are envisaged as restrictions on ownership.
- Property can be passed on from one generation to another.

Ownership in the sense of *dominium* is sacrosanct. It is the right that legitimates all others, while it needs no legitimation.[47]

In the Roman world by the time of the second century and third century CE, large estates known as *latifundia* had been created, secured, and legitimated by the principle of *dominium*. Some of the owners of these estates made the church a beneficiary, and some church leaders were themselves owners of these estates. Legislation in 433 CE provided that the property of any clergy who died intestate passed to the church. A few decades later, in 470 CE, an imperial decree banned the alienation of church property, meaning that the landed wealth of the institutional church was secured for the foreseeable future.[48]

Leading Christian scholars of this period fought against the philosophy of *dominium*. The names of Clement of Alexandria, Basil the Great, Bishop Ambrose, John Chrysostom, and Augustine are familiar to us, but sadly their teachings on this matter are little known.

Clement of Alexandria, born in Athens around 150 CE, was one of the first moral leaders in the church to attack the system of *dominium*. He was an educator and was called "an awakener of souls."[49] He traveled through various regions of the Roman Empire—Italy, Syria and Palestine—before settling in Alexandria, an active center of commercial and intellectual life in the Mediterranean. As Christianity was penetrating ever deeper into the Hellenistic world, the need to train teachers and instruct new Christians in the basic tenets of the faith became more critical. Catechetical schools were established, the most famous of which was the school of Alexandria. In this cosmopolitan city, Avila says, "Clement examined the problem of the relationship between wealth, the social order, and salvation."[50]

Clement focused his teaching on the principles of *autarkeia*, which Avila translates as "self-sufficiency," and *koinonia*, meaning "community."[51] Building on these foundational concepts, Clement created a hierarchy of values, which placed self-sufficiency—meeting basic needs—first. He proposed that since humanity is one race, God wills that we live in community, and everyone in the community should have the means to be self-sufficient. Based on this reasoning. Clement argued that "the ownership of wealth should not mean the right to do with it as one wills. Rather, one should do with it as God wills."[52] Clement taught that we live in community, "*therefore,* everything is common, and the rich should not grasp a greater share."[53] The idea that some should live in luxury while others live in poverty was, for Clement, *atopon*—absurd.[54]

Clement did not teach the renunciation of private wealth, but rather he asserted that "goods are called goods because they do good, and they have been provided by God for the good of all."[55] Thus, he proposed a balance of *autarkeia*—personal independence and self-reliance—and *koinonia*—community. Reliance on these two principles could, he believed, establish a natural threshold for private wealth and ensure that the common good would remain greater than private gain.

Basil the Great became the bishop of Caesarea in the middle of the fourth century.[56] By this time, the Roman system of *dominium* had become more sophisticated and more oppressive, leaving both the land and the peasants exhausted. Village leaders and members of the ruling class acquired title to property and then, backed by the power of the empire, informed the people of the village and the surrounding area that they owned the land. The plebeians (*coloni*) who worked the land were forced to pay patricians who owned the land for the right to work the land. Two-thirds or even as much as three-fourths of the wealth produced went to the owner of the land. In addition, the *coloni* had to pay any taxes that were due and cover any expenses incurred by the owner. The consolidation of wealth, power, and privilege was further protected by laws prohibiting interclass marriage between patricians and plebeians.

Basil attacked this system of dominion in prophetic sermons:

> That bread, which you keep, belongs to the hungry; that coat which you preserve in your wardrobe, to the naked; those shoes which are rotting in your possession, to the shoeless; that gold which you have hidden in the ground, to the needy. Wherefore, as often as you are able to help others, and refuse, so often did you do them wrong.[57]

Ambrose of Milan, the third Church Father of the patristic period cited by Avila, served as the governor of Milan, Italy before he became the bishop of Milan.[58] Writing in the fourth century, Ambrose drew largely on the Bible, Basil the Great, and classical authors for inspiration. He used Christian insights to transpose the insights of Stoic philosophers who held "do no injury to anyone, unless provoked by injury" as the first principle of justice. Ambrose recast this negative notion of justice into a positive concept by maintaining that mercy is part of justice. Whereas the Stoics emphasized the prevention of harm, Ambrose argued that since God created all things and we are all children of God, the first duty of justice is to do good and share our goods. Ambrose deepened this Christian insight further when he cited the Incarnation and made specific reference to the Christian obligation to love others.

John Chrysostom, also a fourth-century figure, was the bishop of Constantinople before he was forced to flee to Antioch, the capital of the Roman province of Syria, where he spent most of his life. Chrysostom denounced the wealthy and called Empress Eudoxia a "Jezebel" who robbed the poor of their lands as Ahab had robbed Naboth. In a sermon on Luke 16, the parable of the Rich Person and Lazarus, Chrysostom said:

> This is robbery: not to share one's resources. Perhaps what I am saying astonishes you. Yet be not astonished. For I shall offer you the testimony of the Sacred Scriptures, which say that not only to rob others' property, but also not to share your own with others, is robbery and greediness and theft.[59]

Like Clement and Basil, Chrysostom affirmed the goodness of creation. He believed that God's intention was that creation was for the benefit of all. He attacked the practice of amassing a fortune and leaving it to one's heirs. In making this argument, he contradicted Roman precept that the possession of property was prima facie proof of ownership. According to Roman law, when ownership of property was contested, the nonowner had to bear the burden of proof. The person who possessed the property in question had the benefit of doubt. In contrast, Chrysostom contended a priori that all property was held in common; therefore, property owners had to show proof that they or their ancestors had not acquired it unjustly. He also argued that use of the wealth of the earth, like the air that we breathe, is a natural and common right of all people. In one sermon Chrysostom asserted:

> We have received all things from Christ. Both existence itself we have through him, and life, and breath, and light and air, and earth…We are sojourners and pilgrims. All this about "mine" and "thine" is mere verbiage, and does not stand for reality. For if you say the house is yours, it is word without

a reality: since the very air, earth, matter, are the Creator's; and so are you too yourself who have framed it; and all other things also.[60]

Augustine of Hippo, the last of the Christian philosophers of the patristic age studied by Avila, began his career in Carthage, moved to Rome for a time, and from there went to Milan, where he became acquainted with Ambrose, who baptized him. Later he became the Bishop of Hippo, a post he held until his death in 430 CE.[61] It is asserted, but not conclusively proven, that at this time six landowners possessed half of Africa.[62] The claim may be an exaggeration, but it is indicative of the concentration of land ownership and the attending problems that Augustine confronted.

The foundation of Augustine's philosophy is that the purpose of life is found only in God. God alone may be loved for God's own sake. Therefore, Avila contends, the true meaning of ownership for Augustine is found in "putting property to right use."[63] People who hold legal title to property are the proprietors, but those who misuse it, or who use it for personal gain while others are barely surviving, are morally bound to make restitution to those whose need is greater. Famously Augustine writes:

> Seek as much as he [God] has given you, and from that take what suffices; other things, superfluous things, are the necessities of others. The superfluous things of the wealthy are the necessities of the poor. When superfluous things are possessed, others' property is possessed.[64]

The revolutionary character of Augustine's teaching is that he stresses that a life of dignity is consonant with our destiny, and this, in turn, calls for a commitment to the proper use of goods for the benefit of all.

These Christian leaders—Clement of Alexandria, Basil the Great, Ambrose, John Chrysostom, and Augustine—wrestled with questions of wealth, property, and justice. They established a tradition that was antithetical to the Roman law of *dominium*. Avila concludes that "The Herculean task of patristic thought was to confront the established ownership concept and stand it on its head."[65] They changed the ownership of property from an instrument of private gain into a public responsibility. They transformed the principle of dominion and exclusion into a principle of inclusion and community building. Drawing on the twin concepts of *autarkeia* (self-sufficiency) and *koinonia* (community), they held that when private property became detrimental to the well-being of the community it was morally wrong. In their teaching, property was not a source of privilege that created division within society but the common bond that held the community together.

If we have the courage to do so, the mainline church today can draw on the theological insights of these theologians of the past and gain much-needed clarity in the present. The twin principles of self-sufficiency and community could guide a church committed to the pursuit of interracial justice in a liberal society. In taking such a stand, the church would present society with a clear path to an alternative future—a future society committed to striving for and securing the well-being of all its people.

Human Rights and Well-being

In addition to repudiating the Doctrine of Discovery and rejecting the theory of *dominium*, I believe that the time has come when those of us in the mainline church must also reform our understanding of human rights. As discussed above, much of our present understanding of human rights is derived from English law. The right of habeas corpus, which safeguards liberty, dates back to 1679. The English Bill of Rights, which establishes the right to free elections, the consent of the governed, freedom of speech, and so forth, dates back to 1689. John Stuart Mill expanded the principle of individual liberty in 1859 with the publication of *On Liberty*.

In this work, Mill famously argued, "the sole end for which mankind are warranted, individually or collectively, in interfering with the liberty of action of any of their member is self-protection."[66] Mill was arguing against the tyranny of the majority on one hand and for the equal treatment of all people in a well-ordered society on the other hand. He was defending the idea that the defense of individual liberty would promote respect for diversity and dialogue, and that truth would emerge from such encounters.

As descendants of Mill, we think of human rights as trump cards of the individual. Human rights adhere to the individual qua individual. They are not granted to an individual by society. Human rights are universal, innate, and inalienable. They protect individuals and minorities from the unchecked and unregulated power of the majority and/or the governing class.

On an abstract level, most white Americans also remain committed to the principle of individual liberty and individual rights. In the mundane world of economics, however, we are leery of the free-rider problem, and we are prone to favor utilitarian outcomes. If some people are denied certain rights for the benefit of the whole society it may be regrettable, but the benefits outweigh the costs. Moral arguments in the form of insisting on the rights of minorities, be it in the Sacred Black Hills or the Oak Flats, do not offer sufficient resistance to a virtually all-powerful economic calculus. Therefore, it is precisely at this point that Christian theology can and must make a contribution.

Crucifixion and resurrection are central tenets of Christianity. Surely cultural genocide and ecological genocide qualify as contemporary forms of crucifixion. We need to pay attention to the root causes of genocide. We have to focus more attention on what happens in the creation of wealth while not ignoring questions about distribution and compensation (which are ways of expressing hope for reconciliation). Concern for what happens in the creation of wealth brings us back to the principle of deep solidarity as a response to the threat of genocide and to the concept of well-being. As an element of justice, the principle of deep solidary has to do with restoring relationships between white Protestant Christians and Native peoples. It (deep solidarity) could reshape our thinking about economics in several ways.[67]

First, deep solidarity is a theology of encounter between members of the mainline church, who have for the most part enjoyed a comfortable standard of living, and Native Americans, many of whom have paid and are still paying a high price for what others enjoy. Deep solidarity teaches us to examine the economy from below, from the point of view of those who have no illusion of equality, just compensation, or equal opportunity. Deep solidarity introduces to us the fuller meaning of what Daniel Wildcat calls "indigenous metaphysics." Unlike Western Christian metaphysics, which Wildcat says tend to "reduce religion to a set of deeply held beliefs unrelated to where people live and how they live," indigenous metaphysics depends on "experiential verification, not logical proof."[68]

Indigenous metaphysics radically changes our understanding of truth. Frantz Fanon graphically describes this experiential, incarnate understanding of truth as truth that is embodied in "the *fellah.*" In Fanon's words: "Now, the *fellah*, the unemployed man, the starving native, do not lay a claim to the truth; they do not say that they represent the truth, for they *are* the truth."[69] Truth for the *fellah* is not an a priori truth. It is not a universal truth. It is not a truth that "grounds" the believer in the air. It is not a cool, controlling truth. Truth for the *fellah* is incarnational, experiential, historical, relational truth. Joerg Rieger says: "This sort of truth cannot be determined once and for all—like the private property of the neocolonialist—but must be discovered time and again along the way."[70] This truth is revealed in the tensions and conflicts of life. Christians are called to be in deep solidarity with Native Americans not in defense of an abstract universal right but because we understand that the God who is met in Christ is present in the struggle to transform situations of subjugation and exploitation and institutions and systems that benefit from these situations.

Second, focus on well-being and the principle of deep solidarity enables us to revalue our values. Whereas free-market theory relies heavily on the abstract law of supply and demand, the notion of market neutrality, and unrestricted self-interest, deep solidarity challenges the calm of market neutrality by exposing the reality of political and economic power to dictate terms of production.

Economist and political scientist Albert O. Hirschman has shown that economists who rely exclusively on conventional market theory tend to ignore the importance of what he calls "exit and voice."[71] Voice is measured by people's ability to participate directly in decision-making. People and institutions with voice have more influence because: (1) voice is information-rich, whereas exit conveys little information beyond discontent; (2) voice is likely to escape from the fetters of cost-benefit analysis; (3) voice is a more complex, less predictable and therefore less subject to control; and (4) voice is the tool most frequently used by activists. Both exit and voice have their place in the political process, but they do not counterbalance each other. Deep solidarity is a way for the church to add its voice to the chorus of Native Americans and others who are already engaged in the political process and to embolden others.

Third, deep solidarity focuses on building relationships that are able to withstand the strain that struggle places on them. Christians experience and practice these ways every week in worship as they pray together, experience forgiveness with each other, and recite the stories of their tradition in song and in ritual. In worship, Christians experience what it means to be part of what biblical scholar Gerhard Lohfink calls a *"contrast-society."*[72] As Lohfink describes this contrast-society, it is an alternative to the violent structures of power of this world. He says that one of the defining characteristics of this alternative society is the "praxis of togetherness" and the "renunciation of domination."[73]

The truth of this alternative society is not enshrined in dogmatic teachings; it is revealed in the experiential metaphysics of life together. Acts of charity are important, but ending the conditions that create the need for charity are even more important. As Gustavo Gutierrez notes, "The absence of sufficient commitment to the poor, the marginalized, and the exploited is perhaps the fundamental reason why we have no solid contemporary reflection on the witness of poverty."[74] Creating a contrast-society with Native Americans in which the quest for interracial justice is normative would be a powerful corrective to the situation Gutierrez identifies.

The apology of the mainline church to Native Americans is a call to action. It is a call to discipleship. It is a call for the reformation of the mainline church that begins with a sustained commitment to a strategy of mutuality, vulnerability, and accountability that brings the predominantly white mainline Protestant church and Native American communities together in dialogue. It is here that we can once again hear and bear witness to the story of the costly hope of the gospel that brings good news of great joy to all people.

A Justice Parable for Today

The Gospel according to Luke tells a powerful story of the day that Jesus came to town (Lk. 19:1–10). News spread quickly. Throngs of people from the surrounding countryside flocked to see him. The main street of town was crowded with people who were eager to catch a glimpse of Jesus as he passed. Zacchaeus, a tax collector and a rich man, was among them. Because he was of small stature, he climbed a sycamore tree so that he could see Jesus. When Jesus came to this tree, he looked up and said, "Zacchaeus, make haste and come down; for I must stay at your house today." So Zacchaeus scrambled down from the tree, and received Jesus joyfully. But when the people saw this, the crowd began to murmur against Jesus, "He has gone in to be the guest of a man who is a sinner."

Neither Jesus nor Zacchaeus backed away from the encounter. Zacchaeus stood erect and promised Jesus, "Behold, Lord, the half of my goods I give to the poor; and if I have defrauded any one of anything, I restore it fourfold." And Jesus said to him, "Today salvation has come to this house, since he is also a son of Abraham."

NOTES

[1]Vine Deloria, Jr., "Religion Today," in *God is Red: A Native View of Religion* (Golden, CO: Fulcrum Publishing, 2003), 30th ed., 292–93.

[2]Ibid., Sacred Places and Moral Responsibility," 282.

[3]Daniel R. Wildcat, "Indigenizing Education: Playing to Our Strengths," in Vine Deloria, Jr. and Daniel R. Wildcat, *Power and Place: Indian Education in America* (Golden, CO: Fulcrum Resources, 2001), 12.

[4]Ibid., 14.

[5]Elizabeth Cook-Lynn, "Reconciliation, Dishonest in its Inception, Now a Failed Idea," in *Anti-Indianism in Modern America: a Voice from Tatekeya's Earth* (Urbana: University of Illinois Press, 2007), 159–70, 165–66.

[6]Ward Churchill, *Struggle for the Land: Indigenous Resistance to Genocide, Ecocide and Expropriation in Contemporary North America* (Monroe, ME: Common Courage Press, 1993), 432.

[7]Elden Lawrence, "Paha Sapa: The Spiritual Mecca," in *He Sapa Woihanble: Black Hills Dream*, ed. Craig Howe, Lydia Whirlwind Soldier and Lanniko L. Lee, (St. Paul: Living Justice Press, 2011), 57–65.

[8]Ibid., 61.

[9]Ibid., 59–60.

[10]See George Tinker, "Pierre-Jean De Smet: Manifest Destiny and Economic Exploitation," *Missionary Conquest: The Gospel and Native American Cultural Genocide* (Minneapolis: Fortress Press, 1993), 69–94. Tinker does not discuss De Smet's discovery

of gold in the Black Hills, but he does give an account of De Smet's ministry, his close ties with the Protestant-owned Hudson Bay Company and the Catholic-owned American Fur Company. Tinker shows that De Smet's short span of mission work among Native Americans was fueled by his economic interests and above all by his belief in Manifest Destiny. He suggests that De Smet's presence in government negotiations with Native tribes was to pacify the them and to facilitate conquest.

[11]"1877 Act," in *He Sapa Woihanble*, ed. Howe, Soldier, and Lee, 165–71.

[12]"1980 Supreme Court Ruling: United States v. Sioux Nation of Indians," in *He Sapa Woihanble*, ed. Howe, Soldier, and Lee, 172–89.

[13]"The Great Sioux Nation: Lakota-Dakota-Nakota," www.snowwowl.com/peoplesioux.html. Accessed January 10, 2015.

[14]Ward Churchill, "The Black Hills Are Not For Sale: The Lakota Struggle for the 1868 Treaty Territory," *Struggle for the Land*, 113–41.

[15]"1868 Treaty of Fort Laramie," *He Sapa Woihanble*, ed. Howe, Soldier, and Lee, 147.

[16]Deloria, *God is Red*, 264.

[17]Brueggemann, *The Land: Place as Gift, Promise, and Challenge in Biblical Faith* (Philadelphia: Fortress Press, 1977), italics original, 4, 5 *passim*.

[18]Fernando F. Segovia, "Introduction: Configurations, Approaches, Findings, Stances," Fernando F. Segovia and R. S. Sugirtharajah, *A Postcolonial Commentary on the New Testament Writings* (London: T&T Clark, 2007), 41.

[19]Pui-lan, "Discovering the Bible in a Non-biblical World," in R. S. Sugirtharajah, ed., *Voices from the Margin: Interpreting the Bible in the Third World* (Maryknoll, NY: Orbis Books, 1995), 293.

[20]Naim S. Ateek, "A Palestinian Perspective: Biblical Perspectives on the Land," in *Voices*, 268.

[21]Brueggemann, *Land*, 125.

[22]I am indebted to Walter Brueggemann's discussion, *Land*, 138–50.

[23]See Michael Nausner, "Homeland as Borderland," in Catherine Keller, Michael Nausner, and Mayra Rivera, eds., *Postcolonial Theologies: Divinity and Empire* (St. Louis: Chalice Press, 2004), for a discussion of "boundaries as zones of contact," 118–32.

[24]Brueggemann, "Hellenization and Syncretism Revisited," *Land*, 158–66.

[25]Ibid., 161–62.

[26]Ibid., 193.

[27]Deloria, "Sacred Places and Moral Responsibility," *God is Red*, 271–86.

[28]Herman E. Daly and John B. Cobb, Jr., "The Religious Vision," *For the Common Good: Redirecting the Economy Toward Community, the Environment, and a Sustainable Future* (Boston: Beacon Press, 1994), 2d ed., 376–400. Quoting Aldo Leopold, they suggest the fundamental principle of a land ethic is, "a thing is right when it tends to preserve the integrity, stability, and beauty of the biotic community," 379.

[29]Cook-Lynn, "Reconciliation," *Anti-Indianism*, 166.

[30]Penny Lernoux, *The Cry of the People: The Struggle for Human Rights in Latin America—The Catholic Church in Conflict with U.S. Policy* (New York: Penguin Books, 1982), 455.

[31]Ibid., 458–59.

[32]From the Oak Lake Writers' Society publication, *He Sapa Woihanble: Black Hills Dreams*.

[33]Louis Hartz, *The Liberal Tradition in America: An Interpretation of American Political Thought Since the Revolution* (San Diego: Harcourt Brace Jovanovich, Publishers, 1955), 140.

[34]Ibid., 5.

[35]Ibid., 55.

[36]Ibid., 62.

[37]Ibid., 17.

[38]Ulrich Duchrow and Franz J. Hinkelammert, "The Case of John Locke: the inversion of human rights in the name of bourgeois property," *Property for People, Not for Profit: Alternatives to the Global Tyranny of Capital*, translated by Elaine Griffiths with Trish Davie, Michael Marten and Páraic Réamonn (London: Zed Books in association with Catholic Institute for International Relations, 2004), 43–76.

[39]Ibid., 47.

[40]Ibid., 47.

[41]Ibid., 49.

[42]Ibid., 52.

[43]C. B. Macpherson, *The Political Theory of Possessive Individualism: Hobbes to Locke* (London: Oxford University Press, 1962), 272–77, *passim*.

[44]Charles Avila, *Ownership: Early Christian Writings* (Maryknoll, NY: Orbis Books, and London: Sheed and Ward, 1983).

[45]Duchrow and Hinkelammert, *Property for People*, 11.

[46]Ibid., 12.

[47]See Avila, *Ownership, 19-21*, and Duchrow and Hinkelammert, *Property*, 11-13.

[48]Avila, *Ownership*, 27.

[49]Material for this section is from Avila, *Ownership*, 33–46.

[50]Ibid., 35.

[51]Ibid., 35–37.

[52]Ibid., 38.

[53]Ibid., 40.

[54]Ibid., italic original, 42.

[55]Ibid., 45.

[56]Ibid., 47–58.

[57]Ibid., 49–50.

[58]Ibid., 59–80.

[59]Ibid., 83.

[60]Ibid., 97.

[61]Ibid., 105–24.

[62]Ibid., 107.

[63]Ibid., 112.

[64]Ibid., 113.

[65]Ibid., 144.

[66]John Stuart Mill, *On Liberty* (New York: Penguin Books, 1980), 68.

[67]I am indebted to Joerg Rieger for suggesting this list. See Joerg Rieger, *No Rising Tide: Theology, Economics, and the Future* (Minneapolis: Fortress Press, 2009), 137–40.

[68]Daniel Wildcat, "Schizophrenic Nature," in *Power and Place*, 48, 53 respectively.

[69]Frantz Fanon, *The Wretched of the Earth*, trans. Constance Farrington (New York: Grove Press, 1968), 49.

[70]Rieger, "Liberating God-Talk: Postcolonialism and the Challenge of the Margins," in *Postcolonial Theologies*, 215.

[71]See Albert O. Hirschman, "Exit and Voice: some further considerations," *Essays on Trespassing: Economics to Politics and Beyond* (Cambridge: Cambridge University Press, 1981), 236–45.

[72]Gerhard Lohfink, *Jesus and Community: The Social Dimensions of Christianity*, translated by John P. Galvin (Philadelphia: Fortress Press, 1984), 56.

[73]Ibid., 99–122.

[74]Gustavo Gutierrez, *A Theology of Liberation: History, Politics and Salvation*. Trans. and ed. Sister Caridad Inda and John Eagleson (Maryknoll, NY: Orbis Books, 1973), 302.

APPENDIX
The Importance of Names

The names that we use to identify each other reflect our cultural practices and entanglements. They may invite dialogue and deepen relationships, or prevent the same. My publisher, editor, and I share a common hope that the title of this book will contribute to what we believe is an urgently needed dialogue and promote the healing of broken relationships. That said, we did not easily agree on the present title on this book.

We questioned if it would be better to use "American Indians" or "Native Americans" in the title and throughout the text. In various drafts of the manuscript I used "Amerindian," "Indigenous People," and "aboriginals." A good friend of mine who is a member of the Muscogee Tribe told me that "Native American" is used more commonly in the academy, while "American Indian" is used more often among themselves. On the other hand, in *An Indigenous Peoples' History of the United States*, Roxanne Dunbar-Ortiz prefers to speak of "indigenous peoples" because she finds "America" and "American" to be "blatantly imperialistic terms."[1] The word "Indian" itself is linked to the European invasion of North America.

Linda Tuhiwai Smith writes in *Decolonizing Methodologies: Research and Indigenous Peoples* that for indigenous peoples naming is how "we put ourselves back together again."[2] Eventually indigenous peoples will come to an agreement on how they identify themselves beyond tribal memberships. Hopefully the nonindigenous community will have the grace and wisdom to accept the identities and names indigenous peoples choose for themselves.

Indigenous peoples often used their tribal identity when speaking of themselves or to others. Whenever possible I have tried to follow this practice throughout the book. However, it was not practical to do this for the title of the book or throughout the text. Finally, we felt we had to choose between "American Indian" and "Native American."

I think for nonindigenous people the present confusion about how best to refer to indigenous peoples is rooted in our colonial history. Since we have not yet come to terms with our own history of anti–Native American attitudes, we do not have the language for a truly multicultural society in which interracial justice is normative.

For example, suppose that "First Nations peoples" is eventually adopted as the most widely accepted way to refer to indigenous peoples.

This name would force nonindigenous people to acknowledge that the people who lived here when the European Christians first arrived lived in communities with functioning governments. They were not barbarians who needed to be civilized. The treaties that the United States made with tribal nations were and are legitimate treaties made between sovereign governments. The implications are rather startling. The Doctrine of Discovery would be no longer valid. The closely related "right of conquest" would cease to be a right. White notions of entitlement would be severely challenged. With the loss of these assumptions, our identity would be compromised. We would have to put ourselves back together.

There are signs that this is beginning to happen. We live in a hyphenated world. We are Afro-Americans, Euro-Americans, Hispanic-Americans, Asian-Americans, and so on. I interpret the presence of the hyphen to mean that we are willing to accept the idea that our identities are relational. As Amartya Sen argues in *Identity and Violence*, we are not "inmates incarcerated in little [identity] containers."[3] We can use our identity to deepen relationships and to nurture community. When we acknowledge that our identities are relational and multidimensional, we reduce our propensity for violence against the Other and open up new possibilities for the creation of a people-oriented society in which interracial justice is normative.

This leads back to the title of this book, *Native Americans, the Mainline Church, and the Quest for Interracial Justice*. We settled on this title not because it is the "best one," but because we wanted to strongly connect the first words in the title "Native American" with the last words in the title "Interracial Justice" and to define the role of the church in this context.

NOTES

[1]Roxanne Dunbar-Ortiz, *An Indigenous Peoples' History of the United States* (Boston: Beacon Press, 2015).

[2]Linda Tuhiwai Smth, *Decolonizing Methodologies: Research and Indigenous Peoples* (London: Zed Books, 2012).

[3]Amartya Sen, *Identity and Violence* (New York: W.W. Norton, 2006).

Index

Scripture Index